"Amber takes us along with her in her journey to simplicity using the book of James as our guide. Insightful. Warm. Challenging."

RUTH GRAHAM, author of *Forgiving My Father, Forgiving Myself, An Invitation to the Miracle of Forgiveness*

"This astounding trip through the book of James is a journey every believer in Christ must take. It's an excellent resource, contemporary, relevant, and practical, painting the simplicity of God's ways of putting iron in our hearts so that we can live a life of faith to His honor in our accomplishments."

REV. JOHNSON ASARE, founder of Center for Good News (Tamale, Ghana)

"Left to ourselves, we overcomplicate even the smallest of decisions, and even more so the larger, more complex crossroads of life. Amber has written a clear, succinct, and practical guide using the wisdom of Scripture that will aid the busiest of us in finding a necessary simplicity in our everyday lives."

GABE TURNER, founder and lead pastor of The Point

"*Finding Simplicity* is a fantastic and inspiring book that I wish I had read when going through the most difficult time in my life as a refugee. I was touched and impressed by how Amber was able to connect with anyone who has gone or is presently going through pain and difficult times in their lives. This is a

powerful book that helps readers find peace through Christ. I encourage you to get more copies to share with others who are going through life's challenges."

ELIZABETH FAHN WEEDOR, founder and executive director of Petals of Hope International, speaker, and author of *Out of the Ashes: My Journey from Tragedy to Redemption*

"*Finding Simplicity* provides a deep well of knowledge and wisdom that gives Christians the understanding of how to live a simple life in a complex modern world. Amber skillfully maneuvers through the book of James with an impressive depth of insight and profundity. She strengthens her case by providing a treasure trove of real-life experiences and creative illustrations that keeps the reader mesmerized."

OLIVER L. ASHER, president of Advancing Native Missions

"Have you ever wanted to take all the complexity in your life and just—cram it through a filter? To simplify things? In this uplifting and beautifully written book, Amber walks us through how we can find simplicity in our lives, using the book of James as the rock-solid foundation. I found myself wanting to re-read the chapters as they are packed with so much wisdom and challenged me to reflect upon every area of my life, my very *walk*—with the Lord—and the impact it has for His Kingdom."

JONATHAN E. HICKORY, veteran police officer, chaplain, and author of *Break Every Chain*

"For the many years I've known Amber, she has always been so passionate about helping others simplify their life. Her journey through the book of James not only simplifies the Scriptures but brings meaningful and practical applications to your heart and your hands. For any believer who wants to find the answers to less worry, less anxiety, less busyness, less stress, and less complexity in the day to day, let Amber share with you the process of living like Jesus in this overly complicated world."

DAVE HERRING, executive pastor of The Point and author of *Father in the Wild*

Finding
Simplicity

Learning to Live like Jesus in the
Midst of a Complicated World

AMBER PARKER

Carpenter's Son Publishing

Finding Simplicity

© 2020 Amber Parker

All rights reserved. No part of this book may be reproduced or transmitted in any form or by any means, electronic or mechanical, including photocopying, recording, or by any information storage and retrieval system, without permission in writing from the copyright owner.

Published by Carpenter's Son Publishing, Franklin, Tennessee

Published in association with Larry Carpenter of Christian Book Services, LLC
www.christianbookservices.com

Scripture taken from the NEW AMERICAN STANDARD BIBLE®, Copyright © 1960,1962,1963,1968,1971,1972,1973,1975,1977,1995 by The Lockman Foundation. Used by permission.

Edited by Lee Titus Elliott

Cover and Interior Design by Suzanne Lawing

Printed in the United States of America

978-1-949572-83-4

To JoAnn

Your challenge, "You need to write," came at just the right time. Thank you for believing in me!

Contents

Introduction   Finding Simplicity 11

Chapter 1   A New Perspective. 15

Chapter 2   Growing Up. 25

Chapter 3   Asking God 35

Chapter 4   The Danger of Doubt. 43

Chapter 5   The Blame Game 51

Chapter 6   The Key to Growth 61

Chapter 7   Looking in the Mirror. 69

Chapter 8   Stop Judging. 77

Chapter 9   Taking a Step. 87

Chapter 10   The Power of Words 97

Chapter 11   Making Wise Choices. 107

Chapter 12   God First. 117

Chapter 13   The Healing Power
of Community 127

Chapter 14   Releasing God's Power 139

Chapter 15   Your Impact. 147

Finding Simplicity

Simplicity—the state of being simple, uncomplicated, or uncompounded. -Merriam-Webster

You don't need me to tell you life is complicated.

We live in a world filled with problems much weightier than any of us can wrap our minds around—poverty, genocide, refugees, sex trafficking, natural disasters, and starving children.

On a more personal level, we face unplanned challenges—health crises, financial strains, employment struggles, loss of loved ones, or any number of trials beyond our control. There is also the chaos of day-to-day demands—a full schedule, interpersonal tension, projects that demand our attention, and internal questions and frustrations.

Amid this complexity, most of us are longing for a simpler life. One with less confusion and greater clarity. Fewer questions and more answers. Less mess and more order.

Lately, it seems there is increasing discussion in regard to decluttering our lives. You don't have to look far to find a method that promises to help revolutionize the way you live. You can try minimalism or the Marie Kondo tidying-up principles. Or perhaps you prefer to implement a time-management strategy or buy a fancy planner that promises to make you more productive.

Although following these methods can help to reduce clutter and bring a level of organization to our lives, unfortunately, they cannot promise freedom from all complexity. Despite our best efforts, challenges will continue to assail us. And often, when these situations arise, they reveal another type of chaos—one that runs even deeper—the chaos of the soul.

Many times, our reactions to challenges are less than gracious and can intensify the complications of a situation. We might overreact to or attempt to avoid a problem altogether, or perhaps we place unnecessary pressure on ourselves to fix things.

As tempting as it is to want to blame the chaos for the way we act, in reality, our actions flow from our hearts. I have found that even if my house is clean, I have prioritized my schedule, and I have a list of goals in place, I can still feel unsettled. Often when my life appears the calmest externally, I may find myself the most restless internally.

If we are seeking external solutions to simplify our lives, we will always fall short. The good news is the Bible offers a better way—the way of Jesus. Instead of adding complexity to an already complicated world, we can choose a simpler path by purposefully looking to Christ and following His lead.

Jesus' approach to God and life stood in striking contrast to that of His contemporaries. The religious people of Jesus' day had made following God extremely complicated. The God they were worshiping was hard to reach, difficult to understand, and tough to please.

Jesus was altogether different. When He talked about God, He made sense. He didn't speak in complex thoughts and sentences but in plain words with relatable stories, using simple illustrations anyone could understand. Most important, Jesus taught not only that man could know God but also that God could change any person's life.

When Jesus walked the earth, He did not succumb to its chaotic pull. Instead, He moved through life purposefully, with order and intent. I love how John Ortberg describes Jesus as "often busy, but never hurried."[1]

> **We find simplicity when we learn to live like Jesus lived.**

The same type of purposeful life that Jesus lived, He offers to us. But this simple path is only available one way— through following Him. Jesus' brother James learned this truth well and wrote a letter that is now part of the Bible. In his writings, James goes straight to the heart of the issues we face: hard times, lack of faith, immaturity, listening to God, unhealthy speech, decision making, sickness, and much more.

Over the years, as I have studied through James both personally and in small groups settings, I can truly say my life has changed. James's firsthand knowledge of Jesus and His teachings is powerful, introducing us to a new manner of living and inviting us to embrace a different perspective than what the world offers. In direct contrast to overcomplicating things, James calls us to a simple yet profound way of thinking. The truths contained within his writings challenge us to implement practices that will transform our personal lives, our walks with God, and our relationships with others.

I pray, as we study through James together, you will open your heart and allow God to lead you into a life of simplicity with Jesus.

CHAPTER 1

A New Perspective

*Few conditions are more unique to a believer's experience and
peculiar to the world than a joy that defies our pain.*
-Beth Moore, *Living Beyond Yourself*

It has been said that you are either just coming out of a trial,
heading into a trial, or are in the midst of a trial. The first time
I heard these words, I responded negatively. My mind pro-
tested, "Well, that is a pessimistic view of life. That certainly
can't be true." Now, many years later, though I still find these
words to be less than encouraging, I know from experience
there is a lot of truth to them.

Maybe, like me, the topic of trials is not your favorite conversation piece. You might even be wondering why I would
begin a book with such a heavy thought. The truth is that,
regardless if we do our best to make wise decisions, to put
things in order, to seek God, and to treat people fairly, we cannot prevent difficulties from coming our way.

If we genuinely want to learn to live like Jesus, we cannot

wait for things to be trouble free. While problems may seem like a hindrance, it is our ability to process and to interact with our trials that may very well determine the course of our life.

In the opening words of his letter, James addresses the challenging circumstances his readers are facing. Listen to what he says: "Consider it all joy, my brethren, when you encounter various trials, knowing that the testing of your faith produces endurance." (James 1:2-3)

Perhaps you are thinking, "What? Did I hear that correctly? How can I think of negative things as 'joy'?"

Or maybe your first thought is, "Sure that is easy for you to say, but you don't know the trials I'm facing. There is no way I can consider them 'joy.' 'Torture,' 'pain,' 'regret,' or 'disappointment' might be the word I would use, but not 'joy.'"

It is tempting to view the problems we experience in our own lives as unique situations. But the people to whom James was writing understood pain and suffering on a deep level.

Let's look at what we know about James's original readers. First off, he writes to "the twelve tribes who are dispersed abroad." (James 1:1) The twelve tribes referred to the Jewish descendants from Abraham. James was writing to a group of people who had once been a flourishing nation but who now had very little. Formerly a ruling force, they were now governed by others and scattered, with no land to claim as their own.

In addition to referring to the declined status of Israel, James was probably also referencing that the Christians of his day had been forced to scatter because of persecution.[2] The book of Acts tells of many Christians who were imprisoned, tortured, and even killed for their faith. This type of persecution caused the Jewish Christians to disperse throughout the region and beyond.[3]

When James is talking about trials, he is clearly not referring to trivial things. He is addressing people who have lost friends and family, refugees who have fled their homes and who are trying to start over in a new place. It is to these people he speaks the message, "Consider it all joy."

Through partnering with Advancing Native Missions, a global-mission organization, I have had the privilege of meeting men and women who have faced tremendous persecution for their faith. When I read James's words, I think of their stories and the deep joy they have found in following Jesus, despite the trials they have experienced.

One powerful example is my friend I'll call Aya. Using her real name is too dangerous, since she risks her life every day simply because she is a Christian.

Aya grew up in a nation that adheres to strict cultural and religious practices. As a teenager, she was raped and soon discovered she was pregnant. She kept the pregnancy a secret as long as she could, because, in her community, as the woman, she would be held responsible for this act. Her fears proved correct. When her pregnancy became obvious, Aya was taken to the center of the city, where she was publicly beaten, then imprisoned.

Because of her weakened physical condition, Aya went into labor prematurely. She was briefly placed under house arrest so medical care could be provided for her and her baby. Miraculously, both Aya and her newborn daughter survived. It was during that short period of internment that Aya met a man from South Africa. At the time, this introduction did not seem significant, but it would turn out to be a miracle, too.

Following her return to prison, this man sent her a package. Aya was surprised to receive an unopened parcel. It was common practice for a guard to open and to search all packages before stamping them with a seal of approval, but this package arrived intact. Inside, she found a T-shirt, money to buy food, and a Bible.

When Aya saw the words "Holy Bible," her first reaction was one of anger. How could this man place her in danger of even more punishment? It was illegal to possess a Bible! Knowing this, Aya decided to burn the forbidden book before she was caught. As she was hiding in the bushes, preparing to light the Bible on fire, a thought struck her: "I have never seen or read this book, and no one I know has ever seen this book. I am already a sinner, so what is one more sin?"

With that, she opened its pages. The first words she saw came from Psalm 139:13: "For You formed my inward parts; You wove me in my mother's womb."

The words resonated so strongly with Aya that she could not bring herself to burn the Bible. Instead, she began to read and study it every day. Then, one night, she had a dream. In the dream, she saw a bright light and a door. Understanding that she must either choose to walk toward or away from its brilliance, Aya moved forward. As she did so, she heard a voice say, "I will never leave you or forsake you."

When Aya shares her story, at this point, her face radiates with joy, and she will tell you, "That voice was the voice of the Lord Jesus. And, from that moment, He has always been with me."

Like the believers to whom James was writing, Aya's choice to follow Jesus brought many additional trials. She was imprisoned yet again, this time for her Christian beliefs. When she refused to renounce Jesus, she was tortured. Eventually, she was denationalized — stripped of her home, her family, and her country. But if you ask Aya if it was worth it, she will emphatically answer, "Yes."

Aya experiences joy, even in hardship and persecution, because she has found a higher purpose—knowing Jesus. Since she can no longer return to her homeland, she has become a missionary in a nearby nation, where she ministers to a community of people from her native country. Though her life is threatened, she is often mistreated, and she sometimes feels alone, Aya continues serving Jesus.

> We find simplicity when we choose joy in every situation.

I realize that most of you reading this book have never been imprisoned or had your life threatened because of your faith, but you, too, face trials. And just like Aya and the Christians of James's day, you need to know that joy is possible, regardless of your circumstances.

Even while working through the final edits of this book, I am facing what James refers to as "various trials." Each of these trials, whether big or small, presents a choice. I can choose to respond with joy or turn toward anxiety and complexity.

A few months ago, I took a trip to Nicaragua. During the travel home, our team experienced flight delays, nights in airports, and just an overall long journey. Being run-down from travel, shortly after returning, I contracted pneumonia. This illness led to two weeks in bed and many more weeks of operating at less-than-full capacity. Even now, my body is weak and worn. Facing this health challenge, I find it easy to worry about all the things I am unable to do. I wonder why my body is struggling to heal, and I become discouraged. These thoughts take me to a negative place, compounding my physical struggle by adding mental and emotional stress.

Last week, I learned that someone I love and care about is walking through a tragic situation. Even as I am typing this, I am overwhelmed with sorrow, as I consider what this person is facing. In moments like these, I struggle with feeling helpless, hopeless, and fearful, and I wonder why God would allow such a horrific circumstance.

On a much smaller scale, last week, I also found out that an event I am organizing had the venue fall through. Now that the planning process has taken an unexpected turn, there are many questions to answer and decisions to make. It would be easy to give in to frustration, to feel overwhelmed, or to want to pass off responsibility. But each of these responses will only serve to complicate the situation, rather than moving toward a solution.

Of all the trials I am walking through right now, the one that has most threatened to steal my joy is a financial one. Even though this area is certainly not my greatest concern, it is one where I have allowed myself to spiral to an unhealthy place. In addition to numerous medical bills from my bout with pneumonia and other health issues, I have had to make several repairs around the house. Simultaneously, I am struggling to raise funds for an upcoming mission trip. My financial shortcomings have surfaced with feelings of isolation and disappointment. Instead of trusting God, my mind quickly develops worst-case scenarios and fills with doubt and insecurity.

Thankfully, in each of these situations, James's invitation to "consider it all joy" continues to speak to my heart and mind. It reminds me that joy is not only possible; it is also God's gift to me, as I walk through each challenge.

While "joy" is an easy word to say, living out its definition can be difficult. In James 1, the word *joy* originates from the Greek word chara, which means *joy, delight,* or *gladness.* Some Bible versions even translate the word as *pure joy.*

When I was young, there was fleeting popularity of optical-illusion pictures designed for you to fix your eyes on a 2-D pattern until a 3-D image would take shape. No matter how intently I stared or attempted to focus my eyes a certain way, I could never capture the image others so easily seemed to do. My brothers or friends would ask, "Do you see it?" or, "Have you figured it out yet?" Finally, after repeated attempts and failures, I would casually say something like, "Oh, I think I see it," and give up.

At times, James's advice to consider our trials as joy can feel a lot like those optical illusions. We want to believe that God is good and that He is working in our lives, but, no matter how hard we try, all we see are our challenges. We might have people around us who keep asking, "Don't you see what God is doing?" or, "Aren't you amazed how God is using you?" But, honestly, we just don't see it.

So how do we find joy?

The most important thing to note about joy is that it is not something we can create on our own, nor does it come by hard work or mental tricks. Instead, genuine joy comes directly from God. Anytime we attempt to find it apart from Him, we will always fall short.

Like James, the author of Hebrews addresses the question of how we can live the Christian life during hardships. His advice is straightforward. We need to fix "our eyes on Jesus, the author and perfecter of faith, who for the joy set before Him endured the cross, despising the shame, and has sat down at the right hand of the throne of God." (Hebrews 12:2)

Not only is Jesus our source of joy; He is also our example of how to experience it during our most difficult moments. From this verse, we see that Jesus endured the suffering of the cross by focusing on what was beyond that pain to find joy. He had the hope of a greater future. In the same way, we are encouraged to look to Jesus and to realize there is something greater than our present pain.

Often, when we are facing adversity, we get tunnel vision and allow our circumstances to become the defining factor of our lives. We have a hard time seeing anything beyond that moment or situation.

Pondering this reminds me of a time I was hiking through the Blue Ridge Mountains on a trail that started in a wooded area and that quickly made a steep descent. To keep my footing and to avoid snakes and other critters, I intently focused on the path before me. After ten or fifteen minutes of hiking, I glanced up, only to discover a perfect view of a full mountain range right beside me. By concentrating solely on my next step, I was missing the breathtaking view surrounding me the entire time.

In our everyday lives, it's necessary for us to look up, too. Looking up reminds us of how big God is and gives us a new perspective to face our challenges. The Bible tells us: "Don't shuffle along, eyes to the ground, absorbed with the things right in front of you. Look up, and be alert to what is going on around Christ—that's where the action is. See things from His perspective." (Colossians 3:1-2 The Message)

I realize many of you are living with unbelievable pain or seemingly insurmountable obstacles. In these seasons, most of us want a solution, something that can fix, resolve, or remove the problem altogether. But it is right in the midst of your situation—solution or no solution—that God is offering you joy.

To find joy, we have to change our perspective. For you, this might mean the following:

- Praying and asking God for help
- Setting aside time to rest and refresh
- Reading a book or Bible passage that helps you learn who God is
- Committing to stop defining yourself by or equating yourself to the trial
- Spending time with a friend or family member without talking about this particular situation
- Talking with someone in detail about this situation to gain perspective from a different angle
- Journaling and reflecting on your thoughts
- Repeating a verse that encourages you when you are overwhelmed

Every one of us experiences trials, and every trial offers us a choice. We can choose to focus on the negative, or we can determine to find joy by looking to Jesus and following His example. Choosing joy transforms us and allows us to move toward simplicity, embracing the life God has designed for us today, no matter what we are facing.

Reflection:

1. Think of a trial currently confronting you. What would it look like to choose joy here? How can choosing joy simplify your situation?

2. What practical steps will you take to focus your eyes on Jesus today?

CHAPTER 2

Growing Up

Those times when you feel like quitting can be times of great opportunity, for God uses your troubles to help you grow.

-Warren Wiersbe

Have you ever noticed that when looking back at particular seasons of life, we often view ourselves much differently in the present than we did in the previous moments? We might think, "If I knew then what I know now...", "I thought I was so mature," or, "I feel like a completely different person now." As a child or a teenager, we are unaware of the many things we don't know. However, over time, we begin to realize we know a lot less than we once thought we did. Transitioning to adulthood, we face new situations and circumstances. We develop new skills and learn to make decisions on our own. We also form a worldview and gain a better understanding of who we are.

Our growth and development continue, as we walk through life. Even though we may have a hard time seeing it ourselves, when we talk to older people, most of them will be quick to inform us just how much we still have to learn. This tendency to be unaware of our immaturity or of areas in which we could improve or grow is true in our spiritual lives, too.

In the previous chapter, we established that it is possible to find joy even in the most challenging of circumstances. But, still, you might be wondering, *Why?* Why does God allow these circumstances in the first place? If He is all-powerful, can't He just eliminate pain from our lives?

We don't always receive answers to all of our questions, but, in this case, James gives us a glimpse into how God views our trials. Remember James 1:2-3, "Consider it all joy, my brethren, when you encounter various trials, knowing that the testing of your faith produces endurance." He continues, "And let endurance have its perfect result, so that you may be perfect and complete, lacking in nothing."[4]

Every trial you face is designed to produce endurance and to help you mature spiritually. While we are typically most concerned about our comfort, God is more concerned about our growth.

Remember my struggle with pneumonia I mentioned? Without the ability to perform and accomplish things I usually can, I have been forced to rely on both God and other people. I have had to say no to many things, reprioritize, and relinquish control. Through this, God has been showing me that He does not depend on me. I can trust Him even when I cannot rely on my own strength. In a season of physical weakness, I have gained spiritual might and power.

In 1 Corinthians 13, our relationship with God is compared to a man who puts away childish behavior as he advances into adulthood. "When I was a child, I used to speak like a child, think like a child, reason like a child; when I became a man, I did away with childish things. For now we see in a mirror dimly, but then face to face; now I know in part, but then I will know fully just as I also have been fully known."[5]

Some behaviors which are acceptable for a two-year-old are not okay for a twelve-year-old or a twenty-two-year-old. In the same way, until the day we are face-to-face with Jesus, all of God's children should be in the process of learning and growth.

Jesus Himself was described as "increasing in wisdom and stature, and in favor with God and man."[6] Interestingly, the Bible ties Jesus' personal growth to the trials He faced. Hebrews 5:8 tells us that "although He was a Son, He learned obedience from the things which He suffered."

Do you see the connection? Suffering and growth are interwoven.

Most of us tend to want to run away from challenges, but James encourages us to face them with endurance. Why? God has custom-designed a curriculum just for you and your growth, and it cannot be separated from adversity.

If we look closer at this word "endurance," we find it also translates as the word "patience." Patience. Have you ever heard someone say you should never pray for patience? A lady in one of my small groups would always remind people praying for her, "Don't pray for the 'P' word." She knew, from personal experience, that there is only one way to learn patience, and that is from situations that test it. While I don't necessarily recommend her approach of never asking God for patience, thinking of her is a good reminder that God will put situations in our lives to develop the character He wants from us.

Sometimes the easiest way to understand a word is to look

at the opposite of it. So what does it look like when a person lacks endurance or patience?

- They take matters into their own hands or take a shortcut when they get tired of waiting.

- They are usually irritable and say things they later regret.

- They stop short of the goal and are never able to enjoy the desired results of accomplishment.

- They give up when things get too hard.

- They make unwise decisions, thinking they will get ahead in life by short-circuiting the process.

- They give up on people because they are tired of showing love and compassion.

- They live frustrated lives because they never fully realize God's purpose and plan.

Do you see how impatience can lead us away from simplicity by taking already challenging situations and making them even more complicated?

I will never forget meeting a little girl named Angel. I was visiting a church with a friend of mine and ended up helping her in the children's class she taught. It was nearly ten years ago, but Angel's little life made a lasting impression on me. Entering the room, she asked, "What are we going to do?" Each time we began one activity, she quickly inquired, "What are we going to do now?" It didn't matter what the exercise was; as soon as we began it, Angel would ask, "What's next?" Never stopping to enjoy the experience, she was continually ready for the next thing. She was so eager to discover something new that when she received it, she didn't even appreciate it.

The reason I remember Angel so clearly is that as quickly as the unkind thought of, "Wow! This little girl is really annoying," crossed my mind, God showed me Angel was a perfect picture of how I lived my life. I was always looking for something new. The only problem was that I never appreciated what I had received. I wasn't participating in the curriculum God had prepared for me, because I wanted to move on to the next thing, and then the next thing, and then the next thing. In reality, I needed to slow down and pay attention to what was right in front of me.

God's plans for us extend far beyond where we are today, and His curriculum for our growth is often found in the most challenging and demanding situations. In his book *Leadership Pain*, Samuel Chand explores why God allows pain in the lives of people who are serving Him. Chand explains it this way: "He's giving them the experience of pain—opposition, conflict, and resistance—to expand their capacity for more compassion and wisdom than they've ever had before. Difficulties are God's curriculum for those who want to excel."[7]

Without question, most of us would probably agree that we want to excel. The more important question is, Are we willing to take the steps necessary to grow? If you have a goal to become physically stronger, it will never happen if you neglect exercise. Without conditioning your muscles, you will not attain your goal. In the same way, unless we exercise our "patience muscles," we will never grow spiritually mature.

James 1:12 states, "Blessed is the man who perseveres under trial; for

> We find simplicity when we see our challenges through God's perspective.

when he has been approved, he will receive the crown of life which the Lord has promised to those who love Him." Don't miss what God wants to teach you today. Often when we can't see clearly, we want to give up. When we don't understand, we want to run away. When the pain is too real, we want to skip ahead. But, just like joy, perseverance is rooted in seeing life from God's perspective.

Thinking back to my early twenties, I remember how these verses in James 1 came alive to me. I had just completed my master's program and was facing the question: What am I going to do with my life? Despite a few degrees, I was not any more prepared to answer that question than the time when I started school. Nonetheless, with great determination, I set out to find the answer. What I didn't realize was that God had a different goal in mind than I did. He was about to use this season to take me deeper in my walk with Him. It was time for me to grow up—not just in the worldly sense of becoming an adult but also in the spiritual sense of learning that God's ways are drastically different than mine.

With the best résumé I could create, I put myself in the job market, all the while knowing God was telling me something other than what I was setting out to do. For some reason, I sensed God wanted me to work in the university office in which I had previously been working as a student. The only problem with that career choice was that it was a student job, and I was no longer a student. Since the message God was speaking to me did not match the circumstances I could see, I plowed ahead on my own.

My stubborn determination brought me into one of the worst times of frustration I had ever experienced. Most doors shut firmly, and the few options that seemed to be opening, I felt God was telling me to avoid. There was one job, in particular, that I wanted and that seemed perfect for me. The interview process lasted several months, and I made it to the last round, only to find someone else was selected.

After receiving the rejection phone call, I remember sitting on the floor in my room, asking God, "Why? If I just want to serve You, then why?"

In response, God spoke to my heart, "If you really just want to serve Me, why are you so upset right now?"

Good question, God! If I had pure motives and just wanted to serve Him, why was my pride wounded? Why was I so unsure and insecure? Well, I certainly wasn't taking James's advice to consider all things joy. Joy comes from knowing God is in control and is working all things for my good. I was just not thoroughly convinced of this truth.

As I continued to search for a job and door after door closed before me, I became even more desperate to hear from God. I needed His direction because I had no idea where to go or what to do. As a planner, this was exasperating for me. I hate not knowing the next step in any situation, and I especially disliked feeling that my entire life was without direction. But it was here in my desperation that God began to speak to me on a new level.

My dependence on God continued to grow, because, as we all know, without a job, there is not an income flow. As a new graduate, my financial reserves were small, and, within a few months, I was at the end of my finances. I was learning to seek God for literally everything I needed, from my rent payment to my next meal.

I finally took a job at a local coffee shop my friend managed. After completing a bachelor's degree and a master's degree, the job wasn't exactly an impressive next step. It was not the kind of thing you can boast to your family and friends about, but I was in the season of God's shaping, and that does not always come in the form we expect.

Like an immature toddler, I continued to beg God for His immediate intervention (otherwise known as pitching a fit). I wanted what I wanted, and I wanted it on my timetable. Just like a toddler, who does not realize there is more to the world than her immediate need, I was engrossed with my desires.

After many months of wrestling, I recall one particular day when I pleaded with God to open doors for me. He responded with a clear answer. Unfortunately, it was not one I liked. It came in one word: *perseverance*. God wanted me to learn to press through difficulties and disappointments. While my goal was finding the perfect job, God's objective was my spiritual growth.

Looking back to my years after college, I can see that God knew when I was first asking Him to open the doors for jobs, I wasn't ready yet. I still measured success on status and achievement instead of spiritual maturity.

As you can probably guess, God did not leave me at the coffee shop forever. After about a year of waiting, learning, seeking Him and the "P" word, God granted me the exact position I had been praying about. But I entered it with a new perspective. Because I had grown up spiritually, I was ready for the next season of serving Him.

Since that time, I have faced trials that are heavier and harder than job searching, but the lesson remains the same. When I think I am more mature than I am, God is willing to put me through the curriculum designed for my growth. Ultimately, He is not nearly as concerned about my comfort or my success as He is about my learning to live like Jesus.

No matter our age, God will continue to give us trials shaped perfectly to help us become more like Him, as we learn and grow, following the footsteps of Jesus.

What if, during these trials, we stopped asking, "Why me?" and started asking, "What?"

What, God, do you want me to learn through this situation?

Reflection:

1. Think of a time God used a trial to help you grow. What did that look like?

2. Now, consider your current circumstances. In what way has God specifically designed a curriculum to help you mature?

3. How can changing your perspective help to simplify a difficult situation you are facing today?

4. What specific steps will you take to partner with Jesus in this time of growth?

CHAPTER 3

Asking God

Christ wants every one of His followers to live lives that reveal His breathtaking ability. But we have to really want and need God enough to activate that power.
-Dick Woodward, *The 4 Spiritual Secrets*

Lacking.

If you were creating a list of the top ten words to describe me, that is one word I hope would not make the list. Yet there are many days this would be the exact word I would use to depict myself. Lacking. Not having what it takes, not measuring up. In over my head.

What about you? Do you ever feel you lack what it takes? Like no matter how hard you try, you will fall short?

Too often, life takes us by surprise. We get into situations we don't know how to handle. We are in a conversation, and we have no idea what to say. We need to make a financial decision. We have to face that same person or circumstance again, even though nothing has changed.

For those of us who understand all too well what "lacking" means, James has some powerful words of encouragement: "But if any of you lacks wisdom, let him ask of God, who gives to us generously and without reproach, and it will be given to him." (James 1:5)

Remember that James has just been talking to his readers about facing trials and about the ways God uses those trials to mature and develop us. It is almost as if he can hear his readers responding: "Okay, James, I get it. God is working in all that is happening in my life and is going to grow me through this. But that doesn't help me know how to react or interact now. I need more than an idea or a concept. I need to know my next step. Where am I to go? What am I to say? Do I stay or walk away? How am I to act? How can I stand firm?"

It is to our practical needs that James speaks a message of good news. No, on our own, we don't have the wisdom to walk through our challenges and trials, but when we are lacking, we have somewhere to go. Or rather, *Someone* to go to—God.

Even as I am writing this chapter, I have a deep sense of lacking the wisdom I need to walk through circumstances confronting me. I think about my friend crying in my arms, as her past decisions seem to be robbing her of present peace. I struggle with how to offer hope and support to another friend whose child may have cancer. I fall short in knowing how to wade through an interpersonal conflict between others, in which I find myself inadvertently involved. I require wisdom for choices, demanding I make them and the ability to navigate a hard conversation I need to have. If I were to use one word to describe how I feel today, it would be *inadequate*.

But you know the beautiful thing about God? Unlike me, He is not deficient. Not only does God ever lack anything;

He is also the source of *every* good thing, including wisdom. Romans 11:33-36 reads: "Oh, the depths of the riches both of the wisdom and knowledge of God! How unsearchable are His judgments and unfathomable His ways! For who has known the mind of the Lord, or who has become His counselor? Or who has first given to Him that it might be paid back again? For from Him and through Him and to Him are all things. To Him be the glory forever."

Just as a nation rich in resources is able not only to provide for its own people's needs but also to export supplies to other countries, so God is also rich in resources. His wisdom is plentiful and endless, because He is the source of it all, and it is from this infinite supply that He offers abundance to us. His provision of wisdom will never be depleted, because it is a part of who He is.

I don't know about you, but wisdom is something I want and need! Thankfully, the person who taps into God's wisdom has access to a full supply, because God never holds back. But sometimes we do. While God's wisdom is *available* to everyone, it is not necessarily *given* to everyone. It is released only to the person who requests it. If we fail to ask God to share His wisdom with us, we shouldn't be surprised to find ourselves lacking it.

In our society, most people give to others on the basis of performance or what they can receive in exchange. This way of thinking makes it easy for us to assume that God gives only to those who deserve or earn His favor, but that is not true. James describes God as giving to us generously and without finding fault. (James 1:5) In other words, God is willing to grant us more than we require and never with judgment.

I wonder how many of us fail to ask God for things we need

because we feel condemned, guilty, or judged. Perhaps we project the rejection we have received from other people onto God. Maybe we realize how unlikely we are to give to someone as undeserving as ourselves, and we expect our heavenly Father to be the same. That is why having a correct view of God is so vital.

When James was describing the generous nature of God, perhaps he was remembering Jesus' teaching from Matthew 7:8-11. Jesus said: "For everyone who asks receives, and he who seeks finds, and to him who knocks it will be opened. Or what man is there among you who, when his son asks for a loaf, will give him a stone? Or if he asks for a fish, he will not give him a snake, will he? If you then, being evil, know how to give good gifts to your children, how much more will your Father who is in heaven give what is good to those who ask Him!"

While we are quick to limit God, He has no such limitations. He gives to us as a loving Father, not hoping to see us fail but to live a successful life.

We find simplicity when we tap into God's supply of wisdom.

When faced with challenging situations, we always have a choice in how we will respond. We can increase the complexity of our circumstances by focusing on what we lack, or we can choose to find simplicity by trusting God to supply us with the wisdom we need. In trusting God, we trade the consequences of confusion and chaos for a way filled with peace and stability.

A few years ago, I read a compelling little book by Emily Steele Elliott called *Expectation Corner: Or Adam Slowman, Is*

Your Door Open? In a few short pages, she uses an allegory to show that many of God's children are missing out on the blessings He has for them. The main character, Adam Slowman, lives in a small cottage on the estate called Redeemed Land. In comparison to others, Adam's cottage is unusually small, dull, dirty, and lacking light. His water supply is almost blocked, and his cabinets have very little food.

Ms. Elliott depicts Adam this way, "Adam lived poor, so to speak, when he might have lived rich."[8]

Those words gripped my heart. When it comes to my spiritual life, how often do I live poor, when I have everything I need to live rich? What about you?

In his letter to the Ephesian church, the apostle Paul addressed this issue. "Blessed be the God and Father of our Lord Jesus Christ, who has blessed us with every spiritual blessing in the heavenly places in Christ."[9] Paul points out that we *already* have every spiritual blessing. Everything we need to live out the Christian life, we possess now.

Going back to the story of Adam Slowman (a story perhaps quite similar to ours), we are told that a flourishing estate surrounded Adam. Many of his neighbors lived in beautiful homes overflowing with abundance.

One day, a messenger visited Adam and asked why Adam was living in such scarcity when the estate Owner would give him everything he needed. The messenger then took Adam to the storehouse of the estate, where Adam viewed a flurry of activity, with petitions coming in and packages going out. He was even shown the "Missed Blessing Office," where unreceived blessings were returned. Most had come back because they were unable to be delivered to the firmly closed houses of the intended recipients. The people who had asked for them were simply not ready to receive the answers to their requests.

The messenger challenged Adam: "You bring discredit on your royal Lord by little expecting and little receiving. Then your petitions, Adam, have had so many 'ifs' and 'buts'—there have come along with them so many 'I don't expects' and 'perhapses,' and so many 'I don't know whether this'll ever get into my Lord's hands, and if it does, I don't know whether He'll hear me,' that they've been—though you mayn't have meant them so—half insults to His goodness."[10]

Could it be that our halfhearted requests, unintentional though they may be, are seen as half insults to God's goodness? Like so many of us, Adam received little because he did not expect to receive anything at all. Prayer lacking the confidence to believe God will work will not bring the blessings we seek. At best, that prayer is mere words and rituals. At worst, it is an insult to our generous Father who longs to provide for our every need.

Praying with confidence means we believe God hears us—not just *sometimes* but *every time* we pray. Whether you need wisdom for a decision, a relationship, an internal battle, or something else entirely, you will find it when you ask God. When we don't ask or when we doubt He will answer, we cut ourselves off from the peace and security God desires for each of us.

If we want to experience God's wisdom, we must shake off our Adam Slowman mentality and be quick to pray with confidence, believing God will liberally give us precisely what we need. For every circumstance. How's that for simplicity?

Reflection:

1. How do you relate to the story of Adam Slowman? Are

you willing to open your door wide to receive all God has for you, or are you hesitant to believe He will be generous in His response to you?

2. What do you think holds you back from asking God for wisdom?

3. Do you think of yourself as being rich in resources or lacking in Kingdom supplies? Why?

4. Currently, in what circumstance or decision do you need God's wisdom? How would tapping into God's provision help to simplify your life in this area?

CHAPTER 4

The Danger of Doubt

God is not only bigger than our hurts but He is also bigger than our mistakes and unbelief—even those things we have brought on ourselves.
-Dutch Sheets, *Tell Your Heart to Beat Again*

Let's be honest together. Think about a time when you prayed, asking God for help, but you never really expected His help to come. Instead of waiting for His answer, you plowed ahead, trying to solve things on your own. Then, maybe you went back to God again, albeit still not believing, only to return to your attempt at rescuing yourself. Perhaps you considered trusting God, but you just couldn't quite let go of control. Back and forth, back and forth. Asking again and again, but never seeing a breakthrough. Asking again and again, yet never finding peace. Just thinking about this spiritual tug of war makes me feel worn out. But, so often, this is how we interact with God. It is no wonder we are worried and exhausted.

James identifies the key to receiving wisdom as a two-part

process. First, we have to ask God for wisdom. Second, we must confidently apply it to our lives. To the person asking for wisdom, James issues the following warning: "But he must ask in faith without any doubting, for the one who doubts is like the surf of the sea, driven and tossed by the wind." (James 1:6)

We find simplicity when we choose confidence over doubt.

God understands our human nature and knows that the simple act of asking is incomplete without our willingness to apply the wisdom we receive. Doubt enters when we fail to trust God. When doubt comes in, we are shutting the door to God's promises and opening the door to questions and concerns, setting ourselves up for failure and filling our lives with uncertainty and instability.

James compares the dangers of one who doubts to a tossing surf. Instead of determining its own course, each wave is subject to the control of the sea's tides. When the wind blows, the wave is helplessly thrown about, powerless to choose its path. It's the same for us if we fail to follow God's direction and instead allow something or someone else to set our course. When we surrender to the tug of our trials, or people, or circumstances, we are left subject to their whims and will find ourselves spinning wildly out of control and overwhelmed by stress.

This analogy reminds me of the story of Peter walking on water. Peter and the other disciples were traveling with Jesus all across Israel. They were working hard, interacting with crowds of people, facing pain and heartache. And they were tired. Can you relate? Walking with Jesus is full of amazing miracles, unexpected opportunities, and incredible challenges, and sometimes we get tired along the way.

This particular day, the disciples boarded a boat and began to cross a lake when, suddenly, what should have been a quiet journey was interrupted by the stormy sea. The men were alert, focused on the storm, when they saw something they had never seen before — a man coming toward them, walking on water. At first, they were fearful, but then the man spoke. The voice was one they knew well—that of their Master, their Teacher, their Leader, their Savior—it was Jesus. When Jesus spoke to His disciples, His words were simple and profound, "Take courage, it is I; do not be afraid."[11]

Sometimes, Jesus appears to us in the most unexpected ways and the most unexpected places, like those when we are focused on the storms of life. Even there, Jesus is present, and His voice is calling to us. I wonder how many times we miss Him, because our eyes are on the wrong things. How often, instead of looking at God, are we looking at our problems?

When Peter recognized Jesus, he impulsively desired to be with Him. Perhaps Peter wanted to be part of a miracle. Maybe he wanted to experience the power of Jesus. Or it may be that Peter just wanted to take a walk with his Savior. Whatever the case, Peter called out for Jesus to command him to come out on the water. And Jesus did so. While all the other disciples stayed in the boat, Peter stepped out and walked on the stormy sea.

Don't miss the power of that. **Peter walked on water.** Walking with Jesus, Peter had the same power as Jesus. Stepping out of the boat and focusing his eyes on the Lord, Peter did the impossible. What about you? When is the last time you stepped out of your boat? What miracles have you seen, as you've followed Jesus? What impossible things has God performed on your behalf? What impossible things are you still expecting Him to complete?

Peter's stint of water walking was short-lived because he got distracted. He realized the storm was still raging. Yes, Jesus was there. But so was the squalling sea. The fear returned, and Peter began to sink. Desperate for rescue, he did the only thing he knew to do; he called out to Jesus. Ever ready to respond to a cry for help, Jesus reached out and held Peter. But Jesus also had something to say to him. Brief and straight to the point, He asked this daring disciple, "You of little faith, why did you doubt?"[12]

It happens to us, too. We step out on faith and see God move. We sense His presence and feel His power. Then we start to look around us and notice the pain, problems, and challenges are still there. Suddenly we begin to focus on what could go wrong or what is already going wrong. Before we know it, we have turned our attention from Jesus, and we have started to sink, choking and sputtering in our circumstances, slipping deeper beneath the surface and becoming closer to being a drowning victim.

When James gives us this description of the doubting person as one "driven and tossed by the wind," he doesn't stop there. James continues with this strong statement, "That man ought not to expect he will receive anything from the Lord, being a double-minded man, unstable in all his ways." (James 1:7-8)

God takes doubt very seriously and will never reward it. He knows doubt will destroy our faith, filling our lives with instability and insecurity, and He desires far more for us than that. God wants us to have peace, steadiness, and a simplicity that can only come from His presence and His wisdom.

I want to speak to those of you who have experienced or are even now experiencing doubt. I'm assuming that's the vast majority of you reading this book. While James makes it clear that doubting will hinder blessings, you must remember that doubt does not have to have the final word. The Bible is full of examples of men and women who overcame doubt by applying God's wisdom.

Remember what happened when Moses was called to speak to the Pharaoh and proclaim the message of freedom for God's people? Moses fixated on the idea that he was not a good speaker. In short, he allowed his inadequacies to consume him to the point that he questioned God's assignment. We might have expected God to agree with Moses and to affirm his lack of talent, but that is not what God did. Instead, God reminded Moses of His power. With that gentle reminder (which, granted, came from the flames of a fiery bush), Moses went from being a scared runaway to becoming a leader of a mighty nation.

What about Esther, the orphaned Jew who ended up as queen of Persia? When presented with the idea that she could petition the king on behalf of her people, her first response was fear. Common sense told her that going before the king could (and probably would) result in death. But when her cousin Mordecai reminded her that God had elevated her to her current position for a purpose, Esther chose to face her fears and to seek God's favor. In turn, God used her to save the Jewish people from annihilation.

Elijah was a man mighty in prayer, and God used those prayers to display His power miraculously to the people of Israel. Despite this, Elijah was overcome by fear when his life was threatened, and he fled to save himself. Instead of continuing to trust God, he became convinced that he was alone, and he allowed self-preservation and self-pity to overwhelm him. God met Elijah in his despair and spoke directly to his concerns, opening his eyes that Elijah was most certainly not alone. After hearing from God, Elijah went back to work as a prophet and raised the next generation of spiritual leadership for his nation.

Then there is Jeremiah, another prophet of God. When God called Jeremiah to proclaim His truths, he made excuses, "I can't speak well," and, "I am too young." But God touched Jeremiah and put His words inside Jeremiah's mouth. For years, Jeremiah delivered divine messages to people who desperately needed a word from God. Even today, his words continue to testify to God's character and to His redemptive love for His people.

Let's return to the story of Peter, the man who faltered on the stormy sea and was rebuked by Jesus for his lack of faith. This very same Peter later preached to thousands of people, explaining who Jesus was. He became a pivotal leader in the early church, an author of part of the New Testament, and he died as a martyr proclaiming his love for Jesus to the end. Why? Because, despite what Peter lacked, he knew Jesus. He looked to Jesus and asked Him for help, and, through the Spirit of God, Peter was transformed.

Just like these biblical figures, God is presenting you with the same choice. Will you give in to doubt, or will you confidently trust Him?

Choosing doubt brings instability not only to our lives but also to the lives of everyone around us. Think about it for a minute. An unstable father brings uncertainty to the entire family. A mother who worries can smother her children and even prevent them from growing into secure and functioning adults. An indecisive boss holds back the whole company from making decisions and moving forward. A friend who overanalyzes and second-guesses herself can be exhausting and will probably drive others away.

On the other hand, a father who walks by faith provides a secure foundation for his family, bringing peace and stability. A mother who trusts God encourages her children to take risks and to believe that God can do amazing things with their lives. A confident boss helps employees to think big and to accomplish their goals. A friend who boldly steps into her calling is energizing and challenges those around her to trust God, too.

Think about what would have happened if Moses had refused to approach the Pharaoh. What might have been the outcome for the Jewish people if Esther had not stood before King Xerxes on their behalf? How would the nation of Israel have been affected if Jeremiah had refused to speak truth against the lies of his day?

It continues to amaze me how God can take the most ordinary people and use them to do incredible things. More than that, God can take the messed-up, broken failures—people who have allowed doubt, fear, and insecurities to overtake them—and move through them, despite their weaknesses.

James's words and these stories of faith challenge me to ponder how quick I am to limit God. I tend to see what I can or cannot do and to forget that God is the endless provider of everything I need to live out His calling.

What about you? What is happening in your relationship with Jesus? Are you sitting in the boat, paralyzed with fear?

Are you debating on whether to step out in faith? Are you walking toward Jesus with your eyes fixed on Him? Or are you focused on the storms of life and beginning to sink in the water?

Wherever you are, whatever the circumstance—Jesus is there. He has something to tell you and to teach you. He is ready to give you precisely what you need, but you have to be willing to take a risk, as Peter did. Are you willing to call on Jesus and to step out of your boat and into the storm with eyes fixed on Him?

Remember that it is not enough to know God's Word. It is not enough to know God can provide. It is not enough to know what you *should* do. You have to live out the wisdom you receive and apply it to every facet of life. Only then, as you learn to live more like Jesus, will you move toward simplicity, finding His strength and peace for every circumstance. Even the hard ones.

Reflection:

1. Are you currently experiencing doubt? What is at the heart of it?

2. Which of the Bible characters mentioned in this chapter do you relate with the most? Why? How does their story encourage you to take a stance of faith in yours?

3. How will you confidently apply God's wisdom to a situation in which you have been experiencing doubt?

CHAPTER 5

The Blame Game

If Satan can get you to believe a lie, then he can begin to work in your life to lead you into sin. This is why he attacks the mind, and this is why we must protect our minds from the attacks of the wicked one.
-Warren Wiersbe, *The Strategy of Satan*

Think back to the time when you were a child. Did you ever deliberately do something wrong, but when asked about your behavior, you quickly shifted the blame to someone else? What was the result? Most likely, if the authority figure realized what actually took place, you increased the consequences of your action by attempting to pass off the responsibility to someone else.

What about as an adult? I am sure all of us have had a time or two (at least) when we have created an enormous mess with our choices. But instead of owning up to our mistakes, we looked for someone else to blame. Instead of making things better, our childish accusations only complicated the situation, and they most likely prolonged the pain and frustrated others in the process.

As we have been working through the book of James, we have established that God desires us to mature and grow. One of the keys to maturity is taking ownership of where we currently are in life, including owning responsibility for our poor choices. Many times, we prefer to deny or ignore our weaknesses over admitting that we have problems. Other times, we choose to play the blame game, looking for someone or something else to pinpoint as the cause of our issues. We will even go so far as to blame God.

In response to this train of thought, James 1:13-14 issues a critical warning: "Let no one say when he is tempted, 'I am being tempted by God'; for God cannot be tempted by evil, and He Himself does not tempt anyone. But each one is tempted when he is carried away and enticed by his own lust." As much as we might like to accuse others, God makes it clear that we are personally responsible for our actions, whether good or bad, right or wrong, healthy or unhealthy.

This toxic pattern of shifting blame goes back to the beginning of time. Remember Adam and Eve? God created them and placed them in the Garden of Eden, with an assignment to tend it. Here in the garden, they walked and talked with God. It was during one of those conversations that God gave them a specific command, "From any tree in the garden you may eat freely; but from the tree of the knowledge of good and evil you shall not eat, for in the day you eat from it you will surely die."[13]

Undeterred by God's warning, Adam and Eve disobeyed. It began with the serpent questioning God's command and tempting Eve. Eve listened to the serpent, saw how desirable the fruit was, and ate it. Then she gave it to Adam, and he ate it, too. Immediately, the couple realized what they had done and hid from God's presence. Still, God could see them and called out to them.

When God confronted Adam with his sin, Adam was quick to shift the blame, "The woman whom You gave to be with me, she gave me from the tree, and I ate."[14]

Do you hear what Adam is saying? *It is Eve's fault*—she is the one who gave me the fruit. And *it is God's fault*—wasn't God the one who put Eve in his life? If God had not placed her there, Adam would not have sinned.

Then God turned to Eve. When asked what she had done, Eve was just as quick to pass the buck. "The serpent deceived me, and I ate."[15]

It was the serpent's fault. Eve claimed innocence. She was not responsible for what she had done, because the deceitful serpent had initiated her action.

Despite their attempts to transfer blame elsewhere, both Adam and Eve were fully responsible for their actions. God would hold each of them accountable for their decision to sin. And just like Adam and Eve, despite our futile attempts to place the blame on God, or on other people, or on the devil, we will each be held liable for our sin, too.

From the Garden of Eden to today, sin always follows the same pattern and yields the same destructive results. James 1:13-15 outlines it this way:

1. **Temptation**: Temptation happens when unhealthy desires and thoughts enter our minds.

2. **Lust**: Lust occurs when we entertain unwholesome desires, allowing a fleeting thought to take root and to

grow into a consuming thought pattern.

3. **Sin**: When our thought pattern moves from our mind into action, we have begun to sin, giving life to our desires.

4. **Death**: The longer we remain in a sin pattern, the more power it holds over our lives. Not only will sin determine the direction of our future; ultimately, if left unchecked, it will also yield death and destruction.

Think about it this way. Let's say I am on a diet, and I am shopping at the grocery store. When I am walking down the baking aisle, I see a box of brownie mix. Since I love chocolate, I conjure up the delightful smell and delicious taste this box can produce. What if, at that point, I tell myself, "I know I am on a diet, and I can't eat brownies, but I will just buy the box and bring it home. I won't prepare it. I will merely enjoy the thought of eating brownies when I see the box in my pantry."

A few days later, I notice the box sitting on my shelf, and, again, I begin to imagine smelling and eating the brownies. This time, I decide, "I know I cannot eat brownies, but that doesn't stop me from making them. I think I will bake these brownies so I can just enjoy the smell."

When those brownies come out of the oven, smelling delightful, what is most likely to happen? My guess is I would tell myself, "Well, I have been doing pretty good on my diet. Now that I've baked these brownies, it won't hurt if I eat just one," which, in turn, would probably lead to me devouring multiple brownies.

Now, think through what led me to eat those brownies. At any point, I could have said no, but, ultimately, the decision to break my diet began in the grocery store when I first saw the box and imagined myself eating the chocolate goodness.

Our sin and the negative consequences of that sin can always be traced back to the moment we first choose to give in to temptation. When we allow our lusts and desires to carry us away, they will always lead down the path toward death.

The Message version explains: "The temptation to give in to evil comes from us and only us. We have no one to blame but the leering, seducing flare-up of our own lust. Lust gets pregnant, and has a baby: sin! Sin grows up to adulthood and becomes a real killer." (James 1:14-15)

It is impossible to grow up and to grow closer to God without taking personal responsibility for where we are and what we have done. Take it from someone who has tried the avoidance route many times; ignoring our weakness and sin only makes life more complicated. Instead of going away, our problems will continue to manifest themselves and will almost always grow increasingly harmful.

> **We find simplicity when we take responsibility for our actions.**

Embedded in the truth that we are fully responsible for our sin is the incredible reality of God's complete sinlessness. Thankfully, He offers us the option to rise above our sinful nature through His power. One of the ways to do so is by implementing James's suggestion: "Everyone must be quick to hear, slow to speak, and slow to anger." (James 1:19) By listening to God and slowing down, we choose the path of life, a route that moves us toward maturity and freedom from sin.

What might have happened if Adam and Eve had paused and listened to God before reaching for the forbidden fruit?

Most likely, they would not have eaten it. God had given them guidance, but they were more focused on their desires than His. In the same way, we would do well to slow down and listen to the truth, choosing to walk in the light of God's Word and power instead of caving to our selfish desires.

Jesus gives us the perfect example of living out this truth at the beginning of His earthly ministry. During Jesus' baptism by John, God confirmed Jesus' identity and mission. What happens next is very interesting. In Matthew 4, Jesus was led by the Spirit into the wilderness to be tempted by the devil.

In this account, there are three specific temptations the devil used with Jesus. The first spoke to Jesus' physical needs. Jesus had just spent forty days fasting, and as you can well imagine, He was hungry. The devil prompted Jesus to use His power as the Son of God to turn rocks into bread.

Instead of fulfilling His physical need and using His power for personal gain, Jesus answered the devil with Scripture, "Man shall not live on bread alone but on every word that proceeds out of the mouth of God."[16] Jesus knew the truth and allowed that truth to shape His thoughts and actions.

Look back to the pattern of destructive behavior outlined by James. What is the first step? Temptation. It is significant to note that although Jesus was tempted, He refrained from sinning. A temptation may be an invitation to sin, but it does not have to result in wrongdoing. Each time our mind fills with negative thoughts, it presents us with a choice—will we entertain these impressions, or will we replace them with the truth?

The devil did not give up easily. Instead, he took Jesus to the highest point of the temple and challenged Him to jump from its heights. What is especially interesting about this temptation is that the devil quoted a verse from the Bible that promises God will send angels to protect His people. In response, Jesus pointed the devil to the full truth of Scripture, "You shall not put the LORD your God to the test."[17]

Temptation can be very subtle, and it often even has the appearance of good. That is why it is dangerous to accept reasoning as truth, without first closely examining it. A large part of temptation begins with thoughts that question the character or the authority of God. In 2 Corinthians 10:5, we are instructed to take every thought captive. Why? Because, just like Jesus, we need to vigilantly remain on guard and filter our response to temptation through the truth of God's Word.

For the third temptation, the devil brought Jesus to a high mountain and gave Him a view of all the kingdoms of the world. The devil then promised that if Jesus bowed down before him and worshiped him, the world would be His. Here, the devil was appealing to the human desire for power, recognition, and authority.

Jesus did not give in to this temptation, but instead commanded the devil to leave Him and quoted God's Word, "For it is written, You shall worship the LORD your God, and serve Him only."[18] Again, Jesus looked to God above His immediate desires.

With each temptation, Jesus had a choice. And, each time, He selected God's way. Similarly, when tempted, we also have a choice. We can give sway to our desires, or we can choose God's way of truth that defeats temptations time and again.

When we ignore the seriousness of sin, we will always find ourselves on the path of pain, trouble, and ultimately destruction. What might seem like a little thing can have significant consequences. No matter how good you think you are doing, adding in something wrong can mess up everything.

Sin not only complicates our own lives; it also affects everyone around us. Think about Adam and Eve. They made a choice that not only negatively impacted their lives but also set all of humanity on a destructive course of sin and death. You and I are still dealing with the repercussions of their decision today.

On the other hand, Jesus refused to deviate from God's call. While giving in to temptation would have destroyed His purpose and had a devastating effect on all humankind, thankfully, Jesus clung to truth. He conquered the devil by choosing the simplicity of God's mission over the promise of immediate satisfaction, quick answers, or temporary fame.

Consider the difference between Adam and Eve's response to temptation and Jesus' response. Adam and Eve chose temporary satisfaction, while Jesus focused on the eternal outcome. They questioned God's Word, while Jesus used God's Word as His defense. While Adam and Eve attempted to shift the blame, Jesus took full responsibility for His actions.

What about you? How are you responding to temptation?

The choices you make will set you on a particular path. Don't deceive yourself into blaming others for your decisions. Your actions develop from what you think and desire, be it good or bad, and you are fully responsible for them.

The next time temptation rears its ugly head, take James's advice to slow down, ask God to reveal His truth about the situation, then listen to and follow what He says.

And whatever you do, don't buy the brownies!

Reflection:

1. Thinking about the three temptations Jesus faced, which one is most relatable to you? Why?

2. Is there a situation where you need to slow down and to ask God to reveal His truth? If so, what is it?

3. Taking responsibility for our actions helps simplify a situation. Is there something you are blaming on someone else that you need to take responsibility for?

CHAPTER 6

The Key to Growth

If we will not take time to study the Bible, we cannot have
power any more than we can have physical strength if we will
not take time to eat nutritious food.
-R. A. Torrey, *God's Power in Your Life*

Recently, God used a little boy named Hunter to teach me a valuable lesson, while I was instructing our church's two-to-five-year-olds. This particular day, I gave a preface to "The Shrink Song." If you are unfamiliar with this tune, it has a simple message: "If you read your Bible and pray every day you will grow, grow, grow; but if you don't read your Bible and pray every day, you will shrink, shrink, shrink."

During my song introduction, Hunter was watching and listening with a confused look on his face. Suddenly, he blurted out, "No, I don't think so." I could tell that he was not trying to argue but that he honestly wanted to understand. From his experience, reading your Bible and growing did not connect.

After singing, we moved into our lesson focusing on how

God loves us all no matter what, even when we make mistakes. I could see my little friend was continuing to listen, processing his thoughts, and wanting to ask questions. When group time ended, all the children returned to their classrooms. But Hunter remained seated on the rug, his head resting on his knees.

Settling beside him, I asked what he was thinking. Hunter shared how he reads his Bible, but he still gets upset. Sometimes he even yells. Keep in mind that this little guy is only five years old but that he is quite serious about growing. We had a conversation about how he can pray to God any time, even when he is upset, and that God loves him unconditionally. But, still, his question remained, "Do I really grow when I read my Bible?"

Hunter's question is one I have asked before, and I am guessing most of you have, too. We want to know: *Why don't I see more growth in my life? Why do I still get angry? Why do I mess up so often? Why can't I get it together?*

Sitting there with Hunter, I was trying to see the message of "The Shrink Song" through a child's eyes. The lyrics make it sound so simple; read your Bible, and you will grow. Maybe Hunter was thinking of physical growth. If so, you don't see that every time you read your Bible and pray. However, I believe he was looking for spiritual growth, and, in reality, you don't always see that, either.

Thankfully, God gave me a simple analogy to share with my young friend. I asked Hunter if he ever needs to get new shoes because his feet are growing. Hunter nodded. Then I asked him if he ever actually sees his feet grow. This time, he shook his head no. I explained that, in the same way his feet are growing, regardless if his eyes can see it happening, when he reads his Bible and prays, he is growing, too.

While there are times we see rapid spiritual growth, most often it comes slowly and steadily, similar to a young child's body maturing. Even if you sit for an entire day to watch, you can't physically see a child grow. But consider the time when you have not seen a toddler for a few months. After a time of separation, his or her physical and developmental growth is apparent.

If asked if we are growing spiritually, we might give the same answer as my little friend, "No, I don't think so." Since we can't necessarily see growth as we go about our daily activities, our progress seems slow. However, over time, if we are consistently following God, studying His Word, and listening to Him, we will change.

James puts it this way: "But one who looks intently at the perfect law, the law of liberty, and abides by it, not having become a forgetful hearer but an effectual doer, this man will be blessed in what he does." (James 1:25) Reading God's Word has the power to change us, but only if we move beyond merely hearing the words and begin to apply them to our lives.

Society tells us the Bible is irrelevant. Culture declares that truth is relative or that we can write it according to our whims. Because of this, we must have certainty in our belief about God's Word.

One of the best ways to understand and to have an accurate view of the Bible is to consider how the Bible explains itself. Looking to Scripture, here are some primary things we learn:

- Scripture is God-inspired and equips God's people to accomplish the things He has called us to do. It is useful for "teaching, for reproof, for correction, and training in righteousness."[19]

- Scripture is alive. As a sword cuts through the body, God's Word pierces the heart, revealing our thoughts and motives.[20]

- Scripture is meant to be contemplated day and night. When we meditate on God's Word and carefully follow His teaching, we are promised to have success.[21]

- Scripture demands careful consideration. If we don't pay attention, we will begin to drift away from God.[22]

- Scripture will survive every test, because it comes from God.[23]

- Scripture is complete and perfect. It has the power to restore anyone and can make even the most simple-minded wise.[24]

- Scripture brings delight. Fruitful seasons will follow those who plant themselves firmly in God's Word. Even if we experience barren times, deep roots will keep us stable.[25]

Jesus often used the phrase, "He who has ears, let him hear." It reminds me of the idiom, "In one ear and out the other."

Jesus knew some people would hear His words only on a superficial level. They might think He told compelling stories, but they would never apply the truths He was speaking into their lives. While their physical ears were hearing, their spiritual ears were deaf. In other words, Jesus' teaching was for the people who desired to listen and to change.

My pastor, Gabe Turner, says it this way, "Hearing God's voice always means listening and obeying."

Jesus emphasized the importance of this truth in an analogy depicting the difference between people who hear His words and act on them versus those who hear His words without making any life application. In Luke 6:47-49, both groups are compared to men building houses. The listeners are like a man who dug deeply and laid a foundation on solid rock. Those who ignore the truth are like a man who built on a sandy surface, neglecting a foundation.

Both of these builders faced a terrible storm. It is not difficult to figure out what happened to each home. Of course, the man who laid a solid foundation had a house that stood firm. In contrast, utter destruction was the result of the man who took the shortcut.

> We find simplicity when we listen to and obey God's Word.

As we have already established a few chapters ago, all of us encounter storms in life. While we cannot control the intensity of the disturbances, we can control how prepared we are to weather them. Listening to and obeying God's Word equips us to endure life's storms instead of collapsing beneath them.

Let's look at one more illustration: In Luke 8:4-15, Jesus tells of a farmer who went out to plant crops. As the farmer spread the seed, it fell in a variety of places, and, depending on where it fell, it generated different responses. Here are the results Jesus described:

- Some seed landed on the road. This seed was either crushed by people's footsteps or was carried away by birds. It never made it into the ground, and so produced no harvest for the farmer.

- Other seed fell on rocky soil. Even though this seed penetrated the ground and produced a few plants, the plants soon withered because the dirt did not contain adequate moisture for them to grow.

• Still other seed went to the ground covered with thorns. While some plants grew, they were quickly choked out, bearing little return for the farmer.

• Lastly, some seeds fell into fertile soil. Unlike the rest, this seed grew successfully, producing a bountiful harvest.

Jesus then explained that the seed in this story represents God's Word. Notice that, in each scenario, the farmer did the same thing. He scattered seed with the potential to yield a successful crop. What was the difference? It was the ground where the seed had fallen. Do you see the connection? Each one of us has been exposed to God's Word, the truth with the power to change lives. What we do with that truth determines the extent of the harvest it produces. Do we have "ears to hear"?

God's Word is powerful, and when we read it, it speaks to us. His words are given for interaction and relationship, revealing who He is and showing us who we are. His words give us hope, provoke change, and, perhaps most important, they draw us closer to God Himself.

Many of us long for a less-complicated life, while, at the same time, ignoring what God has to say. We are stressed about many things yet turn everywhere but to God's truth for solutions. We are frustrated by our lack of progress, all the while claiming we are too busy to read our Bibles. Or when we do read the Bible, we give in to worry and doubt instead of applying God's principles to our lives.

Confusion, chaos, frustration, and stress are not the life that God has designed for you. On the contrary, He longs for you to experience peace, joy, contentment, and simplicity. But you will only find this life when you live God's way.

Jesus said it well: "Enter through the narrow gate; for the gate is wide and the way is broad that leads to destruction, and there are many who enter through it. For the gate is small and the way is narrow that leads to life, and there are few who find it."[26]

Some of you reading this book have spent a lifetime examining God's Word, while others of you may have been intimidated by the thought of studying the Bible on your own. No matter where you are in your journey, the key to your spiritual growth lies in hearing God's truth and putting it into action.

So what does it look like to listen and to obey? A few keys to remember are as follows:

1. **Read the Bible**. Change always begins with truth. You cannot become a doer of God's Word without learning what it says. Set aside time to read and study regularly.

2. **Go slow**. It's no secret that we live in a fast-paced world. Often, we attempt to squeeze God into our busy schedules by spending a few minutes with Him, before rushing on to the next thing. But if we genuinely want to know God and His Word, we have to devote quality time toward it. Slow down, and allow yourself to absorb the truth He desires to speak to you.

3. **Listen openly**. It is tempting to try to make God's Word affirm us and our plans for life. To experience transformation, we must be willing to listen to Him, even if what He says might not be what we want to hear.

4. **Be practical**. Listen for God to speak to you. When He shows you something you are to do, don't complicate things. Take an immediate step of action.

5. **Keep going**. Being a doer of God's Word is not a one-time choice. We have to keep listening, learning, and walking forward, with determination every day.

My friend Hunter posed a challenging question: "Do I really grow when I read my Bible?"

Spiritual growth, like physical growth, is not instantaneous. It stretches beyond a moment and takes place over the long haul of changing seasons. We cannot give up when life becomes difficult. We cannot stop trying, even if we grow weary. Instead, we need to step back and look at the whole picture. We have to continue to read God's Word and talk with Him, as we invite Him to change us bit by bit, day by day. Strengthening yourself in God, you will find, just as the children's song says, "... you will grow, grow, grow."

Reflection:

1. How are your ears? When you hear God's Word, do you ignore it, or do you put it into practice?

2. While listening to and obeying God's Word can bring simplicity to our lives, it can be difficult. What is your most challenging barrier to putting God's Word into practice?

3. If you had to rate the soil of your soul, what type would it be? What steps can you take today to cultivate your heart to receive God's Word and to produce a bountiful harvest?

4. Which of the five keys is the most challenging for you? What changes do you need to make to move forward in your understanding of God and His truths?

CHAPTER 7

Looking in the Mirror

If my private world is in order, it will be because I absorb the words of Christ into my attitudes and actions.
- Gordon MacDonald, *Ordering Your Private World*

"Prove it!" How many heated discussions come to a climax with the utterance of these words? It is one thing to have an influential verbal argument, but words alone are rarely enough to be convincing. Your logic might sound good, but most people don't believe things until they see the proof. Since words can be twisted, arranged, and manipulated to make a convincing point, we have to move beyond mere beliefs and into demonstrable reality. For someone to adopt a new idea, to change sides, or to yield to another person's line of reason, one almost always needs proof.

In no area is this truer than in our Christian walks. It is one thing to say you believe God but another to live as if you do. It is one thing to talk about God but another to let His power change you. It is one thing to proclaim you love God but another to openly display that love.

James challenges his readers, "Prove yourselves doers of the word, and not merely hearers who delude themselves." (James 1:22) Just as in any other area of life, if we want people to believe our faith is real, we must live it out tangibly. Hearing or dialoguing about God is not enough. Faith is rooted in action, and God's presence is best displayed when His people put His Word into practice.

So how do we know if we are genuinely listening to and living out the Word of God? How do we prove our faith is real?

Let's start with a simple analogy. When was the last time you looked in a mirror? Chances are that it hasn't been long. Most of us look in the mirror daily, at the very least. Such was not the case for me during one of my travels abroad. Since my place of lodging had no mirrors, other than the camera mode on my phone, I hadn't looked at myself too closely. When we reached the airport for our flight home, I visited the restroom with another lady from my team. It was there I caught a glimpse of myself in the mirror and noticed my curls were running wild. When I commented on how my hair was having a crazy day, my friend laughed and informed me my hair had looked like that the whole trip. Without a mirror, I had not had an opportunity to assess myself and make any necessary fixes.

Because a mirror reflects our actual image rather than the appearance we have created in our head (be it good or bad), looking into it allows us to make adjustments. If we have food in our teeth, we can remove it. If our hair is out of place, we can comb it. Taking note of our reflection, we have an understanding of who we are.

Just as we do before a physical mirror, we must gaze into

God's Word and see our spiritual reflection to know our true selves and to make needed adjustments. James compares looking in a mirror and applying truth this way: "If anyone is a hearer of the word and not a doer, he is like a man who looks at his natural face in a mirror; for once he has looked at himself and gone away, he has immediately forgotten what kind of person he was." (James 1:23-24)

Most of us are familiar with the fairy tale "Snow White." For me, one of the most vivid scenes from that story occurs when the queen peers into the mirror and asks the question, "Mirror, mirror, on the wall, who is the fairest one of all?"

When she makes this inquiry, she wants only one answer—herself. But one day, she receives the surprising response that there is another young woman who is now the "fairest one of all." I think a lot of us are like that queen. We are looking at God's Word for affirmation of what we want to hear instead of looking for truth and the accompanying opportunity to grow and to change.

Following Christ is more than an intellectual exercise. Listening to good teachers or reading the Bible and other Christian literature doesn't necessarily mean we know God. If we read His Word and walk away without applying the truths we have learned, we may feel temporarily better or boost our morale, but, in the long run, nothing has changed. According to James, we are only deluding ourselves.

God desires that we look into His Word with honest intent, but doing so is not always an easy process. If you only glance at something, you may fail to remember all the details, but when you study it, you will understand it more fully. Just as some of us have physical features we would like to change, when we look closely at our soul through the mirror of God's

Word, we may notice things we don't particularly like. We will see some adjustments we need to make or the things we wish were different. But we will also find grace. We will know God's unconditional love and witness His healing power at work, as His Spirit transforms and changes us.

> We find simplicity when we take time for honest evaluation.

Looking in the mirror is not something we do once a year or even once a week but is something we do every day, sometimes multiple times. In the same way, we need to be consistently in God's Word, looking intently, and seeing our true reflection. Doing this involves not only an honest assessment of our weaknesses but also the positive changes we are experiencing in our lives. A lack of personal evaluation will ultimately lead to frustration, and, over time, it will create a gap between who we say we are and how we are living.

So when was the last time you looked in your spiritual mirror? Do you know who you are in God? Do you notice the things God is doing in, around, and through you? Do you recognize the purpose He is calling you to fulfill? Are there adjustments you need to make? Or are you oblivious to your true reflection, as I was on my mirrorless trip?

James 1 ends with a spiritual checkpoint for those who consider themselves to be followers of God. Here, he offers simple truth, alongside specific ways of measuring spiritual maturity.

When I think of checkpoints, I think of flying. And let's be honest: airport security checkpoints are a hassle. They are usually slow, invade your privacy, and force you to rearrange things, and, at times, they can be intimidating. Regardless of how you feel about them, you are not going to fly without being subjected to them. You can plan your itinerary, pay for your ticket, even arrive at the airport, but until you proceed through the checkpoint, you are not a legitimate passenger.

Security checkpoints ensure you are who you say you are. Without a ticket and a proper ID, you will never board the plane. These safeguards also verify you don't have any of the wrong stuff with you. You won't be making it on board if you insist on bringing liquids, weapons, or other contraband items. If you accidentally packed anything you shouldn't have, the checkpoint will ensure you get rid of it in preparation for your flight.

Every checkpoint also involves screening. Usually, you remove your shoes, place all your belongings on a scanner, then walk through a scanner yourself. If there is any cause for concern, the dreaded pat-down will follow. By the time you have made it successfully through the checkpoint, you have been deemed ready to fly.

I would never suggest the elimination of airport security, no matter how much I dislike going through it. Despite the inconvenience, it is necessary for the safe passage of all. In the same manner, spiritual checkpoints are essential, too.

Most of us would prefer to avoid spiritual checkpoints for the same reasons we want to circumvent airport security—it slows us down, it makes us uncomfortable, it forces change, and it can be intimidating. But we need these checkpoints to verify that our Christian identity is matched by our behavior, ensuring we remove any unhealthy or questionable patterns from our lives.

James 1:26-27 challenges: "If anyone thinks himself to be religious, and yet does not bridle his tongue but deceives his own heart, this man's religion is worthless. Pure and unde-filed religion in the sight of our God and Father is this: to visit orphans and widows in their distress, and to keep oneself unstained by the world."

As we go through this spiritual examination, we need to look at a few things:

1. **Are we saying unnecessary or harmful things?** Unhealthy speech has no place in our lives. If it is there, we need to remove it. Think about the words you have spoken recently. Were they helpful or hurtful? Did they build up or tear down others? Did you need to say them, or would it have been more beneficial to keep your mouth closed?

2. **Are we taking care of those in need?** Orphans and widows share the common trait of having lost family members; they are alone. Following God gives us a heart for people who are suffering and lonely. When was the last time you gave sacrificially? Have you been spending time with someone who needs to know others care? Whose burden have you lessened?

3. **Are we staying pure?** We live in a crazy world, but we are called to be set apart. We should be changing the world instead of allowing the world to change us. Where do you focus your thoughts? Are your automatic reactions generally positive or negative? What is your world-view? Are your thoughts pure and in keeping with God's Word?

Moving forward in our walk with God will sometimes require that we get uncomfortable. It means we have to examine every detail of our life, removing certain items along the way. But when doing so, we have to keep the end in mind. The checkpoint is not the final destination; it is only a stop in the journey. Our goal is to walk faithfully with God and to reflect Him to the world around us.

Eugene Patterson says it this way: "Christians don't simply learn or study or use Scripture; we assimilate it, take it into our lives in such a way that it gets metabolized into acts of love, cups of cold water, missions into all the world, healing and evangelism and justice in Jesus' name, hands raised in adoration of the Father, feet washed in company with the Son."[27]

God's Word is transformational, calling us toward love. A love that changes us, and, through us, changes others. It is only as we embrace this process of transformation and growth that we can follow the simple path of Jesus and bring His love to those in need.

Reflection:

1. Taking time for honest evaluation simplifies our lives, but claiming to follow God, while choosing to live our own way, only increases life's complexity. If our faith is not genuine, we will find ourselves working hard to keep up appearances but continually falling short. In what way do you see this happening in your life?

2. What is God showing you as you look into the mirror of His Word? What adjustments or changes do you need to make?

3. Which of the three checkpoints from James do you need to pay the most attention to right now?

4. What is one specific thing you will do to make a positive step in your spiritual life today?

CHAPTER 8

Stop Judging

*Love is a weapon that can shatter division
and rebuild what has been broken.*
-Jentezen Franklin, *Love Like You've Never Been Hurt:
Hope, Healing and the Power of an Open Heart*

Not too long ago, I had a few extra minutes before my next
appointment and decided to grab some coffee. Ahead of me
in the drive-through was a car heavily decorated with bumper
stickers. While waiting for the line to move, I read the various statements. It didn't take long for me to observe that this
individual had a drastically different viewpoint from mine. I
found myself thinking how little the driver and I had in common, and I presumed that if he knew what I believed, he probably wouldn't care for me much.

When I pulled forward to collect my order, I was told, "The
man in front of you paid for your coffee." Driving off, I experienced a variety of emotions. I was surprised and blessed
but also convicted for my thinking. I don't ever remember

a stranger buying anything for me. But this person (about whom I had formed preconceived notions) had shown me unexpected and undeserved kindness.

I was immediately reminded of the admonition James gave to the church: "...have you not made distinctions among yourselves, and become judges with evil motives?" (James 2:4) God spoke to my heart and revealed how quick I am to judge others. I make assumptions on how people think, what they believe, and how they act, forgetting that every person is both created and loved by God.

When I am judging others, I am not reflecting their characters but displaying my selfish and sinful instincts. As God's children, we are called to love Him and to share that love with others. We cannot accomplish that purpose when our hearts and minds are full of self-centered thinking, unfair expectations, uninformed opinions, or biased criticism.

James puts it this way: "If, however, you are fulfilling the royal law according to the Scripture, 'You shall love your neighbor as yourself,' you are doing well. But if you show partiality, you are committing sin and are convicted by the law as transgressors. For whoever keeps the whole law yet stumbles at any one point, has become guilty of all." (James 2:8-10)

Judging others is just plain wrong, and God takes it very seriously. Often, Christians try to justify certain behaviors. We think that if we can explain our motives, it makes our attitudes okay. But that is not the case. If we are not thinking and acting out of love, we are guilty of showing partiality and judgment.

My experience at the drive-through was a good reminder that I have no way of knowing what is in the mind of another person. I cannot see that person's motives; I can only examine my own, to determine if I am reflecting God's love.

Looking more closely at the situation James was addressing in chapter 2, we understand the church of James's day was making distinctions between the rich and the poor. The church was dishonoring those who had less financial resources, discriminating against them, while at the same time treating the rich with favoritism.

The church's bias would play out something like this: If a man wearing fine apparel walked into a church, he would receive a seat of honor. Because of his wealth and status, he would be shown reverence and treated with extra care and concern. At the same time, if a man dressed in ragged clothing came to that church, he would be overlooked. Often, the poor man would either not be given a seat or be seated in a place indicating his lower status.

James classifies this improper treatment as showing "personal favoritism" (James 2:1). In his commentary on James, John MacArthur explains that the term "personal favoritism" has the literal meaning of "lifting up someone's face, with the idea of judging purely on a superficial level, without consideration of a person's true merits, abilities, or character."

Showing personal favoritism is not limited to the church of James's day. It may look different to each of us, but I am sure we all have countless stories of how "personal favoritism" has affected our lives, whether we were the ones judging or the ones being judged. Prejudices create barriers, add complexity, break down communities, and destroy individuals.

Whether we want to admit it or not, we have a way of categorizing others. Even as I write that, a few of you might find yourself feeling defensive, but stick with me for a minute. This categorizing can be useful when cleaning out a closet, organizing schedules, or making decisions. But it is not so helpful if we attempt to do the same with people.

If any two of us worked together to tidy up a closet, we would take a different approach. We might vary on our view of what to keep versus what to remove. We may disagree whether items should go on hangers or on shelves, in what order things should be arranged, or even what belongs in a closet.

In the same way, we all view people differently, be it in terms of race, gender, age, status, or nationality. Each of us has a filter through which we consider or categorize others, which, in itself, is not wrong. The problem James is addressing occurs when we place people in particular categories, while at the same time determining them to be of more or less value because of that categorization. Acknowledging that someone is unique from us is not bad, but assigning their value on the basis of that distinction certainly is.

In reflecting on my own life, here are a few ways I have seen personal favoritism lived out:

Preferences: We stereotype people according to our observations. We make assumptions that may or may not be true, on the basis of how people dress, the things they do, or where they live. Doing so erects barriers between groups who have more in common than they may realize, but, because of certain behaviors, choices, or attire, they segregate.

This segregation is especially prevalent in high school cliques that inevitably pervade social interactions (and that unfortunately follows many of us into adulthood). My friend Pam and I are a perfect example of this mistaken categorization. Before we became friends, I knew Pam only from church activities. She was a part of the in-crowd at youth group, and I was not. It is safe to say that I was not impressed by this group and had no plans to befriend any of its members. I later learned that she and her sister had heard I was smart, and I didn't think they would like me, either. Despite our initial reactions to each other, we became friends in high school, went on to be college roommates, and remain friends to this day. Contrary to our skewed views of each other, God saw the lifelong friends we would become. Had we not been willing to move past our false assumptions, we would have missed out on a beautiful friendship.

Gender: The Bible teaches that God created men and women in His image. While the genders certainly have some distinguishing characteristics, we are 100 percent equal before God. Unfortunately, throughout our society and the world at large, many women are treated as less than their male counterparts.

On a personal level, I have had my leadership challenged, received less recognition, and have had my judgment questioned solely on the basis of my gender. But my experience with gender discrimination is very minimal compared to that of my friends from other countries. Some were beaten simply because their husbands saw them as property. Others were denied education, while still others have been raped and sexually mistreated. Countless females live virtually unseen, because their society places little or no value on women.

However, let me point out that gender bias is not one-sided. It is not uncommon to overhear women complaining, derogatorily uttering the word "men" with an eye roll. Instead of judging fairly, we demean one another, blaming an entire gender for the faults we have seen in a few.

Race: Growing up in the Southern United States, I have seen the racial tension between African Americans, Caucasians, and Hispanics that is undeniable. It plays out in the educational system, in the workplace, and within the neighborhoods of our country, stirring a general sense of mistrust. While some work to build unity across racial barriers, others hold a deep-seated hatred displayed through bullying, violence, and various forms of discrimination.

In 2017, I saw this tension vividly revealed, as I watched my community in Charlottesville, Virginia, take center stage in national news. White supremacists marched on our local university campus, carrying torches and chanting, "You will not replace us," and, "White lives matter." The next day, a *Unite the Right* rally took place to protest the removal of a statue honoring the Civil War Confederacy. As protesters and counterprotesters gathered, anger, violence, and hatred reigned.

Ethnicity: Even among people of the same biological race, ethnic communities exist. Often, those bonded together through one ethnicity (nationality, culture, language, etc.) experience tension with other ethnicities.

After traveling to Liberia multiple times, I have come to love the nation. Before my first trip, I heard stories from friends and read several memoirs, learning of the pain and struggle behind the two Liberian Civil Wars, which took place between 1989 and 2003. Hostile battles within the country resulted in mass refugees, brutal deaths, child soldiers, raping and pillaging, and the destruction of resources. The atrocities of these ethnic wars have left the country with extreme poverty, rampant corruption, and a deficient educational system with which to invest in the future of the nation. Sadly, Liberia is still reaping the effects of the wars today and is just one country's example of how ethnic hatred has brought division, resulting in pain and violence.

So what is the answer?

What is the solution to the chaos of our world?

How do we overcome the hatred and judgment that both surrounds us and invades our lives?

The answer James gives is simple, "You shall love your neighbor as yourself." (James 2:8).

Please understand that *simple* certainly does not mean *easy*. But it does mean there is only one solution to this great division, be it in our hearts, households, churches, nations, or world. And that is the love of God. While judgment produces separation, love breaks down barriers. When we choose to live in love, instead of bringing confusion and chaos to the world around us, we bring peace and unity.

> We find simplicity when we choose love over judgment.

Here are a few things God's Word teaches us about love:

- Above all other character qualities, we need to clothe ourselves with love. Love brings perfect unity.[29]

- Love is such a basic instruction of the Christian faith that it seems obvious Christians should love each other.[30]

- Eloquently speaking God's message, knowing the deep mysteries of God, or even performing great acts of faith means nothing if we neglect the element of love.[31]

- Love is everlasting. It will never end.[32]

- The genuine test of our relationship with God is the love we have for people. We cannot say we love God and withhold love from others.[33]

- The person who is continually increasing in love will be fruitful and will come to a true knowledge of God.[34]

In Luke 10, Jesus gives the same admonishment as James. When asked, "What should I do to inherit eternal life?"[35] Jesus answers by quoting two Old Testament commandments: "You shall love the LORD your God with all your heart, and with all your soul, and with all your strength, and with all your mind; and your neighbor as yourself."[36] The command to love our neighbor is a central teaching of the Christian faith.

The man who asked Jesus this important question also posed another, hoping to prove his own goodness, "And who is my neighbor?"[37] Instead of giving this man a way out, Jesus shared a story exemplifying a high standard of love.

The story begins with a Jewish traveler who was robbed, beaten, and left for dead, alongside the road. Shortly after, a priest walked by, ignoring the man. Later, a Levite (a man whose livelihood revolved around serving in God's temple) walked past, also disregarding the man. Then a Samaritan man came upon the traveler. This is where the story changes.

It is easy for us to gloss over the significance of what happens next if we neglect to understand the magnitude of division between the Jews and Samaritans. John 4 explains there were no dealings or interactions between these two nationalities whatsoever. Two races, two types of people, two societies who despise each another—this portrays the deep-seated animosity between the Jews and the Samaritans.

The way Jesus' story unfolds, the Samaritan man saw the injured traveler and felt compassion. Unlike the esteemed religious leaders, this man stopped his journey to care for his fellow man. Not only did he bandage the man's wounds; he also took him to an inn and paid for the man to stay there until he had recuperated.

Concluding His story, Jesus asked, "Which of these three

do you think proved to be a neighbor to the man who fell into the robbers' hands?"[38] The answer is evident. The model of a real neighbor was the man who had compassion and acted upon it. It was the man who did not let race, preconceived ideas, or his schedule stand in the way of helping someone in need. Jesus then instructed His listeners to go and follow the Samaritan's example.

Are you catching what Jesus did here? Not only did He give an illustration of sacrificial love; He also elevated a Samaritan man above the religious leaders. Jesus showed that loving God and loving people is not about status or ethnicity, but about obedience. The Jewish men and women to whom Jesus was talking believed they had an elevated position in God's kingdom simply because of their birthright. Jesus countered their belief by showing them that God was not a respecter of persons but that He loved everyone. This same love was to be evident in His children, cultivated and displayed toward all, regardless of their differences.

Just like those whom Jesus was teaching and just like the recipients of James's original letter, we have a choice. We can love people, or we can judge others and commit sin. James makes it clear—if we think we are following God without loving others, we are deceiving ourselves.

It is crucial to note that loving others does not mean we view everyone the same, making no distinction. That is the world's rhetoric—that we should be "color-blind" or all become identical, stripping ourselves of gender, race, and ethnic differences.

In contrast, the Bible teaches that diversity is good. God intentionally designed people to be unique and to reflect His character in a variety of ways. However, God is also impartial in His creativity; His love is not withheld from some and given to others. Through Jesus' love, "there is neither Jew nor Greek, there is neither slave nor free man, there is neither male nor female."[39] We are all one.

It is not hard to see how love can initiate change and bring simplicity to a divided world. Each one of us has the power to embrace unity and to change the tide, as we reflect God's heart with a love that overcomes barriers. But this kind of love is not possible when we allow personal preferences to cloud our view.

What is holding you back from this type of radical love? Is there someone in your life whom you misjudged or a group of people whom you harbor prejudice toward? Consider what it would look like for you to exchange your personal preferences with God's viewpoint and your judgment with God's love.

Reflection:

1. Choosing to respond from a stance of love instead of judgment is not an easy thing to do, but it always simplifies a situation instead of clouding it with mistaken assumptions. How can you allow God to help you overcome the tendency to judge others unfairly?

2. Is there someone specific you need to release from your judgment? How can you take steps toward doing so?

3. In sharp contrast to the favoritism the world is so quick to display, the Bible teaches that God is impartial. How have you seen God's love bring healing across divisions?

4. To whom do you show partiality? How does this partiality place barriers between you and others?

5. How can you begin to bring unity to your corner of the world today?

CHAPTER 9

Taking a Step

If I ask God to do things I could do for myself,
I am dishonest in my praying.
- A. W. Tozer, *The Purpose of Man*

If I asked you to rate your faith on a scale of one to ten, chances are you would give yourself a low score. Although we are meant to have a vibrant and alive faith, most of us would admit that, more often, our faith seems dull and sluggish. We claim to believe God, yet we fall short in supporting this belief with a life that actively reflects it. If you want to know what you truly believe and value, there is only one measurement—your life.

James tackles this thought in chapter 2:20 by asking, "But are you willing to recognize, you foolish fellow, that faith without works is useless?" and a few verses later states, "Just as the body without the spirit is dead, so also faith without works is dead." (v. 26)

If James's proclamations seem a little extreme to you, you

are not alone. Historically, this section of Scripture has been a source of much controversy. Most famously, the reformer Martin Luther labeled James a heretic on the basis of this portion of text.

Luther came from a religious background that promoted performance-based salvation. After studying the Bible more fully for himself, he arrived at the contrary conclusion— instead of being founded upon human works, salvation is a gift offered by our Creator. Despite our best efforts, good behavior cannot earn salvation, move us closer to God, or entice Him to love us more.

James uses the example of Abraham to connect faith to works, but, in Romans 4, Paul uses Abraham's example to teach that faith is not dependent on our labors. How can our faith be disconnected from our efforts while, at the same time, directly linked to them?

It is not my intent to wade into a theological argument or to stir up controversy, but wrestling with the issue of faith is real. If you could see inside my mind, you would recognize my continual struggle with the questions of faith—not necessarily with what I believe but with how I know whether or not I am walking in faith. As a person who likes to get things done, I worry that I will rush ahead of God, but I also fear that I will incorrectly hear God or miss out on opportunities.

Here are just a few examples of questions I wrestle with, to which some of you may relate:

- Can I take action and still be depending on God?

- How do I know if I am listening to God or if I am imposing my ideas on God?

- What does it mean to wait on God?

- When I don't see anything happening, does that mean I heard God inaccurately?

- Why doesn't God answer my prayers?

- When things seem to fall apart, does that mean I don't have enough faith?

- What if I step out in faith, only to discover I was wrong?

Going back to how our faith can be disconnected from our efforts yet directly linked to them, we see this is not an either/or scenario but a both/and one. When interpreting confusing parts of the Bible, it is wise to consider what remaining Scripture has to say about the same subject. Thankfully, God's Word has a chapter dedicated to the topic of faith, beginning with the following definition: "Faith is the assurance of things hoped for, the conviction of things not seen." Biblical faith is a deep confidence in God and an understanding that there is more to life than what we can see with finite eyes.

If you continue to read Hebrews 11, you will find story after story of men and women demonstrating vibrant faith. All of them had a dependence on God and His power stretching well beyond the circumstances of their lives. All of them were prompted to action by their beliefs. Their testimonies stand as proof that faith is not about human strength or effort but that it is an act based on trust in God.

James's claim that "faith without works is dead" is not meant as an invitation to boast about how good we are. Instead, he is genuinely asking: *How do I know if I have faith?*

Here are a few key points James gives to help us answer that question:

- **Faith is more than words.** James's example is

straightforward. What if you see some people in need of food and clothing, but, instead of giving them physical provision, you simply greet them and wish them well? Your words do nothing to help them. They are still hungry, and their clothes are still old and worn. In the same way, a faith not backed with action is meaningless.

- **Faith displays itself through works.** James makes a sobering point. Even demons believe in God, but this belief does not bring about a life that honors Him. Faith is a display of what we truly believe, not just an acknowledgment of God's existence. In other words, our lives should be radically changed on the basis of our worship of God.

- **Faith without works is dead.** James points to Abraham, the father of the Jewish nation. Abraham did not just believe in God; he also acted on that belief. His "faith was working with his works." If Abraham had merely claimed to believe God but never followed it up with movement, his faith would have had no practical value. The only way we know he was a man of faith was by the action paired with it.

Several years ago, my friend Autumn asked me to speak at a women's conference she led. Each year, she would prayerfully choose a theme verse, and each year the theme appeared to be anointed by God. This year was no exception. There was only one problem. When I heard the selected topic, I felt unqualified to teach about it. Even though I would not have admitted it at the time, I wasn't even sure I believed it applied to my life. I knew it had to be true, because it was part of the Bible, but, in practice, it seemed far from reality.

What verse so unsettled me? Joshua 1:3, "Every place on which the sole of your foot treads, I have given it to you, just as I spoke to Moses."

Maybe this particular statement doesn't mean much to you, but it stirred something in me and set me on a journey toward a more active faith. This verse immediately reminded me of my days as a student at Liberty University. Over and over (and I seriously mean over and over), I heard Dr. Jerry Falwell Sr. share the story of the founding of Liberty University. Now, I realize Dr. Falwell is a controversial figure for some people, but one cannot deny that he was a person of great faith and vision. As a young man, he founded a church that expanded into a college and that later became a world-class university.

According to Dr. Falwell, one day, he walked the property where Liberty University now stands. As he did so, he claimed the words of Joshua 1:3, believing God would give him every place his foot touched for the church and the university. Most people thought he was crazy, but Dr. Falwell believed that God had promised him the land. He acted on his faith and saw the words from Joshua come to pass in a tangible and personal way. God provided the property, and, today, Thomas Road Baptist Church, Liberty University, and Liberty Christian Academy rest on that very place. The ground walked and prayed over was claimed for God's vision, and, year after year, that vision continues to expand and to grow.

As I prepared for my teaching on Joshua 1:3, I realized that I wanted to have this type of faith, but my conviction seemed a lot less vibrant than Joshua's or Dr. Falwell's. Honestly, it often appeared the things I was believing God for were either delayed or denied. I didn't experience the breakthrough I was looking for, and I felt disappointed with God, especially when it seemed He didn't come through for me or answer my prayers.

I believe God gave me this particular speaking assignment because He knew I needed a new definition of faith. Up to this point, I had practiced faith as a passive action—it was I waiting for God to work. What I learned from Joshua chapter 1 proved just the opposite: revealing true faith as active and alive. It goes beyond passivity and challenges me to align my life with how God is already working.

The book of Joshua begins at a time of grief and loss. Moses, the great leader of the nation, was dead. As Joshua was processing this painful loss, God spoke to him. "Moses My servant is dead; now therefore arise, cross this Jordan, you and all this people, to the land which I am giving to them, to the sons of Israel."[42]

Joshua is in a particularly challenging place. Not only is he grieving the death of his mentor and friend; he also now has the enormous responsibility of leading the entire nation of Israel. I can only imagine how overwhelming and intimidating his calling is.

If you are unfamiliar with the history of the Israelites, they were known for being difficult, complaining, and rebellious. As Joshua steps into leadership, he finds himself in a place he has stood before, and, the last time he was here, things didn't turn out well.

Forty years prior, Joshua had been sent with eleven other Israelite leaders to scope out the region across the Jordan— the land God had promised to give to His people. Joshua and another faithful man, Caleb, surveyed the property and saw its goodness. They were ready to lead the Israelites to conquer and to claim God's promises. Unfortunately, the other ten men viewed things quite differently. Where Joshua and Caleb saw God's promises, these men saw the opportunity for failure and defeat.

Instead of heeding Joshua and Caleb, the people scorned their advice and rebelled against God. They refused to conquer the land, as they had been commanded. This disobedience caused God to extend Israel's wilderness wandering for an additional forty years.

> We find simplicity when we take steps of faith.

Now that we have the context, let's look at that verse again. "Every place on which the sole of your foot treads, I have given it to you, just as I spoke to Moses." God's instruction to Joshua was basic—he simply needed to take a step forward. Every place where Joshua's foot touched the ground would be the land God's people would inherit.

As I pondered these verses, a phrase repeatedly played in my head: **If you want to claim God's promises, you have to take a step.**

While we should never move forward without first praying for God's direction, once we have received it, we are responsible to act on it. Many times, Christians use prayer as an excuse to stay comfortable, but our immobility does not honor God when He has already revealed what we need to do. We may think we are waiting on God, but, more often, He is waiting on us. If we truly believe His promises, we will take steps toward living them fully.

During my first season of studying Joshua, I knew God had placed gifts in my hands that He wanted to use for ministry, but I was failing to develop those gifts. I soon realized

I couldn't just sit back and wait for everything to happen on its own. To claim God's calling and His promises, I needed to start acting on what I knew.

What about you? What step of faith do you need to take? Your step could be one of the following:

- Finding ways to develop and to use your gifts and talents
- Reaching out to a person to heal a relationship
- Investing financially in your church, a ministry, or a mission
- Stopping an unhealthy pattern or habit that is holding you back
- Moving out of a comfortable place to pursue God's plan

When it comes to fulfilling God's vision and purpose, there is always a gap between where we are and where we want to be. Frequently that gap seems too big to cross, and we can spend much of our lives letting that stop us. Instead of moving forward toward God's calling, we find ourselves standing on the sidelines. In doing so, we are left feeling frustrated and unfulfilled, because we are not living the purposeful life God has designed for us.

Whatever your next step of faith is, I want to challenge you to identify the barriers that are currently holding you back from it. Maybe you are swayed by busyness, lack of empathy, insecurity, internal struggles, deep-seated pain, or doubt.

Now, think about the consequences if you allow these barriers to determine the outcome of your life. What does your future look like? Disobedience? Uncertainty? Are you missing out? Have you walked away from God? Are you disappointing yourself and others? Have you added complexity and frustrations to your life?

Now consider the opposite. What might you experience if you boldly move forward in faith? Obedience? Victory? Growth in your relationship with God? Peace? Simplicity? Confidence? Leadership opportunities? Open doors? Deeper faith?

The real issue is not whether we face obstacles to walking in faith but what we do when we encounter them. Through studying Joshua 1, I realized that fear was my most significant barrier. I was afraid of what people might think, that I didn't have what it takes, or that I might fail. When I was faced with my lack of courage, it was comforting to remember that Joshua was human and experienced fear, just like me.

Moving forward was daunting for Joshua, yet God continually confronted his weakness with the charge to be strong and courageous. Joshua had to shift his thinking from what could go wrong and instead focus on God's presence. The key to facing his fear was knowing God was with him and would continue to be with him every step of the way.

God was calling Joshua to do great things beyond human ability, and He is calling each of us to a purpose beyond our ability to accomplish on our own, too. Every time we step forward in faith, we embrace this call and move along a path toward greater clarity and simplicity. Real faith does not happen overnight but comes day by day—moving confidently, proving what we believe by our actions.

Reflection:

1. On the basis of your current life choices, would you say your faith is vibrant and active? Why or why not?

2. What one thing can you do today to move toward God's vision for you?

3. Taking steps of faith will simplify your life, but keep in mind that "simple" is not synonymous with "easy." Moving forward may be challenging, but doing so is necessary, if you want to see God work in your life. How would taking a step of faith help to simplify your life right now?

CHAPTER 10

The Power of Words

Words which do not give the light of
Christ increase the darkness.
-Mother Teresa

Power. It can accomplish great good or evil. Consider the natural forces of water and fire. Water is essential for life, but it can also cause mass destruction through flooding. Fire is used for warmth, cooking, and creating energy, but when not properly contained, it can also consume buildings, forests, and even human lives.

In the same way that water or fire are mighty forces, the words we say wield power. Solomon, known as the wisest man in his day, said in Proverbs 18:21, "Death and life are in the power of the tongue, and those who love it will eat its fruit." When I consider the implications of this verse, it stops me in my tracks. I can produce both life and death through the words I speak. *And so can you.*

In chapter 3, James illustrates the potency of our tongue by comparing it to a bit in a horse's mouth or a rudder on a ship. While a bit and a rudder are small in size, each determines the direction of something much larger. In the same way, our tongue may be tiny when compared to the rest of the body, but it is mighty.

One of the most dangerous things we can do with power is to overlook the damage it can inflict. James explains it this way, "And the tongue is a fire, the very world of iniquity; the tongue is set among our members as that which defiles the entire body, and sets on fire the course of our life, and is set on fire by hell." (James 3:6) What a description! The words I speak will determine the course of my life, and if those words are negative, I can bring destruction not only to myself but also to others.

If I were to ask you the last time you said something you regretted, you probably wouldn't have to think back far. If we are honest, most of us have a long list of ways we have complicated our lives through our words. Here are just a few examples to which you may relate:

- Blurting out the frustration we meant to hold inside
- Lying to make ourselves look better or to keep ourselves safe
- Accusing someone else of something we know is our fault
- Raising our voices or yelling at someone who does not deserve our anger
- Using sarcasm to cover up how we genuinely feel
- Speaking about people behind their backs
- Name-calling or negative characterization of others

As a Christian, there is no other area in which I have grown as much as in my speech. When I was in college, an honest assessment of the words flowing from my mouth would have included such descriptions as "sarcastic," "biting," "immature," and "shallow."

During this season, a brave friend sat down with me and shared her observations about the impact of my words. She explained that even though she knew I cared about people and had the heart to serve God, the way I communicated was creating a barrier for me. Not only were my tone and words holding people at a distance; worse yet, they were tearing down and hurting others. While I wanted to help people and share God's love, my words were setting me on a course in the opposite direction. My friend's loving confrontation was a defining moment for me.

Our words are an indicator of our spiritual maturity. As we grow, our speech should be continually changing. Jesus explained that our words flow from our hearts. In Luke 6:45, He says, "The good man out of the good treasure of his heart brings forth what is good; and the evil man out of the evil treasure brings forth what is evil; for his mouth speaks from that which fills his heart."

As much as we want to blame our words on our circumstances or other people, the reality is that they are shaped by one source—our heart. Just as experiencing physical heart problems may find us submitting to a stress test to determine the cause of the issue, our circumstances serve as a stress test to reveal the condition of our spiritual heart.

If you are like me, there are times you may tell yourself you are doing great, when, in reality, you are filled with negativity, judgment, or hopelessness. During those times, I usually attempt to plow through and to pretend everything is okay, but, eventually, what is inside my heart comes out. I justify my unkind words with excuses—*I am tired; they understand where I am coming from; we all have our moments; anyone would be frustrated with this situation.* This list could go on and on.

If I continue to ignore the seemingly small comments, before too long (and usually with surprising force), words flow from my mouth that I immediately wish I could retract. What was harbored in my heart is now out in the open and has hurt someone I care about. If only I had stopped to work on my heart earlier, I could have avoided a lot of pain.

As Jesus reminds us, our speech is a direct reflection of who we are. When our mouth spews angry words, gossip, complaint, or grumbling, it is an overflow of our heart. The same is true when we speak lovingly and kindly. Those genuine and positive encouragements come from a healthy heart in line with God.

In James 3:9-10, we are encouraged not only to bless God with our words but to bless people, too. It is not enough to merely remove unfavorable speech from our lives; we also need to use our words to speak a blessing. Words spoken at the right time in the right way are powerful. I love how Proverbs 25:11 states it: "Like apples of gold in settings of silver is a word spoken in right circumstances." Just as a handcrafted piece is designed and perfectly fit together, words appropriately spoken are a thing of beauty.

Many pivotal moments in my life have been tied directly to what others have spoken to or about me. Words of truth and kindness encouraged me; those of insight and possibility challenged me; words of support and love strengthened me.

Over the past few years, God has been reminding me that just as other people's words have shaped me, my words have the power to influence others. The words I speak are important—when I say them and whom I say them to matters.

I wonder if some of you struggle to believe your words can have such an impact. Maybe you are thinking, "That sounds great," but you don't know the situation I am in or the people I live and work with. Perhaps you don't think anyone will listen to you. Maybe you assume it doesn't matter what you say, because nothing will change. It may be that you have convinced yourself that if you say something, even if it is kind, it will only make matters worse.

I mentioned earlier that I have traveled to Liberia. During my most recent visit, I helped lead a women's conference with a team from my church. As I prayed over this opportunity, I felt prompted to share a message on the power of words. But as I prepared this lesson, doubts ran through my mind. Even though I believe God will fill us with His words and use them to change situations and lives, I wondered if the women I would be speaking to would accept this. Or would my lesson seem shallow or uninformed to those who had experienced the hardship of a civil war? Would this teaching fall flat when heard by women who had been raped and defiled, most of whom have little value in their society and are unappreciated and overlooked?

Our theme for the conference was Proverbs 4:23: "Watch over your heart with all diligence, for from it flow the springs of life." God reminded me this truth is for everyone. No matter our position, status, situation, or circumstances, God's life can flow through us. As I prayed for God to show me how to convey this in a way that related to the women in attendance,

He directed me to an Old Testament example found in 1 Samuel 25.

Here we meet two people who portray the extreme difference between using foolish words and wise words. The first is a rich man named Nabal, whose name, rather appropriately, means "fool." Then we meet his wife, Abigail. While Nabal is known for his foolishness, Abigail is described as intelligent and beautiful (a description most of us would prefer—smart and good-looking).

To set the scene for the story, we begin with a young man named David, anointed as the next king of Israel. Even though David was chosen to be king, his predecessor King Saul is still reigning over the nation. Because of Saul's reluctance to surrender the throne, David is hiding out in the wilderness, along with a band of six hundred zealous men, who have joined forces with him.

Camped in the same area as the shepherds who worked for Nabal, this ragtag army was tired and hungry. One might expect the soldiers would take whatever they wanted by force. However, despite their need, they did not steal from or cause any harm to Nabal's men. They even went so far as to offer them protection. On the basis of this positive interaction, David sent a few of his men to seek the favor of Nabal and ask for food.

Nabal, true to his name, responds with harsh, cutting words, "Who is David? And who is this son of Jesse? There are many servants today who are each breaking away from his master. Shall I then take my bread and my water and my meat that I have slaughtered for my shearers, and give it to men whose origin I don't know?"[43]

Not only did Nabal refuse David's request; he also insulted

David and accused him of rebellion. Although Nabal had the means to feed these men, he denied them kindness and hospitality, responding instead with hostile and foolish words.

When informed of Nabal's response, David was furious. And by furious, I mean more than just a little ticked off. He was ready to kill, literally. David gathered four hundred of his men and went on the warpath, straight toward Nabal. This scenario perfectly illustrates Proverbs 15:1: "A gentle answer turns away wrath, but a harsh word stirs up anger." In this instance, one man's foolish words provoked reckless behavior in another, resulting in two men acting angrily and impulsively.

Thankfully, a wise servant of Nabal's understood what was happening and reported everything to Abigail. He explained how her husband had answered David's messengers with contempt, even though David's men had shown nothing but respect and kindness toward Nabal's shepherds. He also informed Abigail that because Nabal was such an ill-tempered and worthless man, he refused to listen to reason.

Let's focus on that description of Nabal for a moment. For me, it is a little too relatable. Foolish people think they know everything. They refuse to listen and often speak rashly, without regard to the effects of their actions. Such was the case with Nabal, and now his worthless character was catching up to him. David and his warriors were about to deal with this foolishness once and for all.

Fortunately, Abigail was not like her husband. As soon as she heard the servant's report, she sprang into action. Wasting no time in gathering food and provisions, she rushed to intercept David and his troops. Abigail humbly bowed to the ground and asked to take the blame for Nabal's foolishness.

I wonder what David and his men were thinking. Here is a lovely woman bowing before them, telling this group of angry men she would assume punishment for her husband's deeds. In addition to her boldness of taking responsibility for Nabal's foolishness, Abigail graciously insinuates that the anger and quick temper David is displaying are beneath his character and God's anointing on his life.

Listen to David's response to Abigail's words: "Blessed be the LORD God of Israel, who sent you this day to meet me, and blessed be your discernment, and blessed be you, who have kept me this day from bloodshed and from avenging myself by my own hand."

We find simplicity when we speak life-giving words.

Abigail's wisdom not only saved her household from death but also restrained David from committing murder. She understood the reach of her power and influence and used her words wisely.

Like Nabal and David, you and I can choose words that create turmoil, breed distrust, stir animosity, and bring violence. Or, like Abigail, our speech can **give life, protect, correct**, and **direct**.

- Positive words are **life-giving**. They have the power to change situations. They can invite people toward rest and refreshing, creating a safe place to confide and to share their struggles.

- Carefully spoken words can offer peace, refuge, and **protection**. When others are facing difficult or even dangerous situations, our words can give hope and may restrain someone from harming themselves or others.

- Words of **correction** can help others diffuse the chaos in their own hearts. By challenging them to look inward, we can help to redirect their course.

- Offering wise counsel gives **direction** and helps others focus their lives and accomplish the goals God has for them. Pointing out the the gifts and talents you see in others encourages them to use them, bringing order and a sense of purpose to their lives.

Do you believe your words can change lives? Both yours and those of the people around you?

Remember how James told us our words set the course of our lives? My guess is that every one of us desires a good future. We want to make a positive impact, as we serve God well and love people. And we want to help others to do the same.

So what course are your words setting? Do they match the future you desire? Or are you destroying your future with your tongue?

The weight of your words holds incredible power, my friend. The question is: *What are you going to do with it?*

Don't wait for the opportune moment to present itself; instead, create it with encouraging words. Determine to strengthen and to love the people surrounding you by living with open hands and with a tongue that speaks life and love.

Then watch what God will do.

Reflection:

1. As we've seen with the story of Abigail and Nabal, life-giving words have the potential to create an atmosphere

where people flourish. Words of wisdom and encouragement invite peace and purpose to take center stage in our lives, as we watch God accomplish astounding things through us. On the flip side, harsh and bitter words leave destruction and chaos in their wake. Looking at your own life, are you more prone to act like an Abigail or a Nabal?

2. Think about the words you have spoken in the last week. What do these words indicate about your heart?

3. What holds you back from speaking words of encouragement or blessing over another person?

4. Who do you need to speak life into today?

CHAPTER 11

Making Wise Choices

The doleful reality is that very few human beings really do concretely desire to hear what God has to say to them. This is shown by how rarely we listen for his voice when we are not in trouble or when we are not being faced with a decision that we do not know how to handle. People who understand and warmly desire to hear God's voice will, by contrast, want to hear it when life is uneventful just as much as when they are facing trouble or big decisions.
-A. W. Tozer, *Hearing God*

I tend to overanalyze decisions. You know, when you let things roll around in your brain and consume your thoughts, and every conversation goes back to that same situation or person. When you don't sleep well, and you can't relax because you want an answer.

Even on the best of days, my overactive mind tugs for my attention, but, on the worst of days, it can rule over nearly every thought. When an unexpected challenge arises—whether health, financial, career, personal, or spiritual—I can go from bad to worse in a hurry, as my busy mind kicks into overdrive. Unfortunately, it is not just my thought life that is affected. My thinking quickly overflows into my conversations, my health, my eating habits, and my work life.

The more I focus on wanting to figure everything out, the more quickly I begin to overcomplicate things. I add elements to situations that are not there, and I attempt to project my future. Unfortunately, my anxious state does not usually promote a good one.

That is what happened earlier this year. I was hurt by the choices a friend had made. At first, I ignored the problem, pretending I wasn't affected. However, over time, on the basis of my emotional responses and internal restlessness, it was clear I needed to deal with the situation.

I wish I could say I quickly worked everything out, but that was not the case. I worried, and I believed things that weren't true, as I played out imaginary conversations in my head and walked through scenarios based on fear, not facts. Not only did I doubt my friend's intentions; I even questioned God.

After months of putting myself through turmoil, I finally realized I had a choice to make. I could allow bitterness to take root, or I could look to God for direction. Once I eventually turned to God, I decided to be honest—with myself and with my friend. This decision placed me on the path to peace, restoration, and healing.

What about you? Have you ever struggled with decision making? Maybe you overthink every possible scenario, or perhaps you are too impulsive. You might want to know all the details, or it may be that the details overwhelm you. It could be that you hold back in fear or that you allow fear to rush you into making a careless choice.

Regardless of our approach to life, we are all faced with choices. Often, those choices are accompanied by competing voices, making it hard to determine which voice to listen to. It would be nice if we were given a simple 1-2-3 formula to follow, to ensure success. It would be easy to make wise decisions, if we could see ten steps down the road and know the impact of the choices we are considering today.

Although we will never be able to predict the future, God does give us advice for making decisions. In James chapter 1, we learned the importance of asking God for wisdom, believing He will generously provide it. In James chapter 3, we will focus on how it plays out in our day-to-day lives.

One of my favorite definitions of wisdom is *knowledge applied*. Wisdom exceeds mere intellectual information, giving us the ability to take what we know and to put it into practice. It guides us in making important decisions in our social interactions, in our speech, and in our everyday choices.

The Bible repeatedly emphasizes the topic of wisdom throughout its pages. In addition to James, the entire book of Proverbs addresses its importance. Let's look at a few things it notes:

- Wisdom begins with the respect and awe of God.[44]

- Wisdom should be sought after like a precious treasure.[45]

- Wisdom gained is worth more than gold and silver.[46]

- Wisdom yields pleasant ways, peace, and life.[47]

- Wisdom brings healing and refreshment.[48]

- Wisdom brings favor and good success with God and with people.[49]

- Wisdom keeps us from stumbling.[50]

- Wisdom guards us and protects us from being susceptible to evil.[51]

Proverbs 9 personifies wisdom as a lady with a fortified house filled with good things. She calls out to the surrounding city, "Whoever is naive, let him turn in here!"[52] To all who lack understanding, Lady Wisdom promises provision and direction. Whoever listens to her voice will add value to his or her life, will draw closer to God, and will continue to increase in wisdom.

Interestingly, Lady Wisdom is not the only voice portrayed in this illustration. Lady Folly is parroting her, "Whoever is naive, let him turn in here."[53] Don't miss that Lady Folly is using identical words. The problem is that she is described as "naive" and "knowing nothing."[54] Everything she offers is stolen and temporary. Her wares are appealing to the eye, but they lack substance. Indeed, they are harmful and empty. Her offerings bring short-term benefits but long-term pain.

If you have ever traveled internationally, you know the importance of clean water and the necessity to avoid any liquid that has not undergone proper filtration to remove impurities. While tainted water may temporarily quench your thirst, it can leave you with much-worse problems on your hands.

Too often, we fail to apply this same care to our spiritual life. Just as we would never purposefully consume contaminated water, we should be careful to determine the purity of the counsel we put into ourselves before making decisions. The voices of wisdom and foolishness are always competing for our attention. Both are offering to help us make life choices, but only one gives pure advice. It is imperative to recognize the difference and to choose wisely.

So how do we know when we are making wise choices? James addresses this very topic with his question, "Who among you is wise and understanding?" (James 3:13) Similar to Proverbs 9, James goes on to explain there are two types of wisdom—the wisdom of God and the wisdom that does not originate from God.

The book of 1 Corinthians makes this same comparison, while offering additional insight. Here we are told that Jesus is the "wisdom of God."[55] From this, we know that wisdom is much more than behavior modification or self-enlightenment. It is the very character and nature of God Himself come to life in the person of Jesus Christ. If our choices reflect Him, then we know we are making wise decisions. Conversely, any wisdom originating from a different source is false and will lead us on a path of destruction.

Let's go back to James's question, "Who among you is wise and understanding?" In reading this, we see it as a rhetorical question. Instead of pointing to specific people, James engages his readers with the assumption that they are the "wise and understanding" people. He then encourages them to show their good behavior by their "deeds in the gentleness of wisdom." (James 3:13)

I have to admit that "gentleness" is not the first word that comes to mind when I think of wisdom. The words "brave" or "powerful" might seem more fitting options. But the distinguishing behavior mark here is gentleness. Why? Because wisdom is not displayed in bold decisions, in eloquent speech, or by flaunting its strength. It is not about saving the day or fixing the problem right before our eyes. Wisdom shows itself best by steadily reflecting God in our choices. It is most evident when we are consistently living out biblical truth and peaceably displaying the character of Jesus in our daily lives.

On the other hand, James gives two signs to help us recognize when we are falling into false wisdom. The first element to check for is bitter jealousy. Is the basis for my thinking found in my comparing myself to others or a desire to prove myself? Do I respond with harshness toward people? Do I experience a feeling of lack because of what others have? Anytime our decision stems from a desire to be like someone else or to gain what others have, we are heading toward destruction.

The second element is selfish ambition. The word here for selfish ambition can also translate as *strife*. It is the desire to be at the top; to put yourself first; to have the place of honor or recognition. When we make decisions to elevate ourselves, we can be sure we are en route toward trouble.

James warns: "If you have bitter jealousy and selfish ambition in your heart, do not be arrogant and so lie against the truth. This wisdom is not that which comes down from above but is earthly, natural, and demonic." (James 3:14-15) If bitter jealousy and selfish ambition are present, your thinking is not grounded in God. Rather, it is grounded in wisdom generating from the culture or society, in a personal agenda, or in thought; even worse, it is rooted in evil.

Most of us desire to make good choices and to live a full and happy life. We rarely knowingly choose harm or destruction. The problem is that it can be easy to deceive ourselves. We can become so confident we are correct that it never crosses our minds to question our directions. Recognizing you are wrong takes brutal honesty, not just with other people but also with yourself. Before making an important decision, we need to set aside time for self-evaluation, verifying we are not looking for just affirmation of the answer we wanted.

On more than one occasion, I have used this guide in James to pray through a decision, only to find God revealing a problem with my heart. On one occasion, I needed to decide whether or not to continue in leadership with a particular ministry. Although I felt God telling me to resign, I continued serving. As time passed, I noticed a deep, internal restlessness. Finally, I turned to God and measured my motives against the guidelines from James 3. In doing so, I realized I was holding onto this ministry for all the wrong reasons. I was jealous of friends who had more opportunities than I did, and I wanted both status and recognition. I was on a destructive course of serving myself instead of serving God.

This experience is just one of many times I have wandered the path of jealousy and selfishness. Although the occurrences have looked different, they have all led to the same end. Internal and external chaos has left me floundering without peace or purpose.

James explains it this way: "Where jealousy and selfish ambition exist, there is disorder and every evil thing." (3:16) When we experience restlessness and disorder, it is time for self-examination. A few critical questions to ask are as follows:

- Am I listening to wisdom's voice or the call of folly?

- Am I seeking my desires over God's direction?

- Have I compromised truth in exchange for the world's advice?

- Have I dropped my guard and let evil slip in?

The answers will help us determine our motives and the current course of our lives.

Just as it is imperative to recognize when we are going the wrong direction, it is equally valuable to know when we are on the right path. James 3 continues to outline God's wisdom: "The wisdom from above is first pure, then peaceable, gentle, reasonable, full of mercy and good fruits, unwavering, without hypocrisy. And the seed whose fruit is righteousness is sown in peace by those who make peace." (James 3:17-18)

To ensure we are following God's wisdom, we can apply these elements as a filter:

- **Is my heart pure?**

  Do I respect God and seek to reflect Him with my life? Are my thinking and actions clear and faultless?

- **Am I walking in peace?**

  Are my relationships without contention or strife? Am I directing people to God's redemption by living peaceably with others?

- **Is my behavior gentle?**

  Do I point to God, instead of drawing attention to myself? Am I kind and tolerant toward people, or do I become impatient when I am waiting on God to work?

- **Is my thinking reasonable?**

  Do I listen instead of stubbornly holding to my own way? Does my thinking have order and reason? Can I explain how my decisions connect to God's Word and plan?

- **Am I relating to others in mercy?**

  Am I kind to others and quick to help them? Do I give second chances? Do I reflect God's love and forgiveness in my everyday interactions?

- **Does my life bring about good things?**

  Are my time and energy devoted to things that matter? Am I positively impacting people by the things I do?

- **Am I unwavering?**

  Am I sound in my thinking, or do I waver back and forth? Do I have a clear and confident approach to decision making? Do I feel content with my current place and my future direction in life?

- **Do my words match my actions?**

  Am I honest? Is the person I claim to be who I genuinely am? If people followed me around, would I be comfortable, or would I be ashamed of what they would see?

When we can answer yes to all of these questions, we can walk confidently, knowing we are following the way of Jesus. If we base our thinking and behavior on God's wisdom, our lives bear good fruit. Instead of reaping chaos and confusion caused by false knowledge, God's wisdom yields peace and simplifies our inner world.

> We find simplicity when we recognize and apply God's wisdom.

Even while writing this chapter, I have wrestled between God's wisdom and following my own way. Sleep has escaped me, as I processed through a situation confronting me. Then, I remembered (again) that I am not the source of wisdom. God is. It is not for me to figure out all the details on my own. I needed to tap into the Source.

The book of Luke gives us a strategic picture of how Jesus made decisions. At the beginning of His public ministry, Jesus selected twelve disciples, who would learn from Him and serve alongside Him. The night before He chose these men, Jesus went off to a mountain alone and spent the entire night in prayer. Like our Savior, when making decisions, I need to spend time in God's presence and in prayer, too.

So, this week, I decided to practice what I am writing. I set aside time to pray and to seek God. While my situation has not yet changed, I have. Noting selfishness creeping in, I turned my attention to God instead of myself and the things I wanted. While I was debating giving up or taking matters into my own hands, I was reminded of what true wisdom is. It is peaceable and pure, gentle and reasonable, and it bears good fruit. Today, instead of allowing the pressure of decision making to overwhelm and stress me, I am choosing to honor Jesus. In His presence, I feel the tension release and can rest in His wisdom.

What about you? Are you relying on your own strength or the flawed reasoning offered by the world? Or are you simplifying your life by looking to Jesus as your source of wisdom?

Reflection:

1. Think about a time when you made a decision based on bitter jealousy or selfish ambition. What did that look like? What was the result?

2. Are you currently wrestling with a difficult decision? Use James 3:17-18 to evaluate whether or not you are listening to God's wisdom.

3. How can applying God's wisdom to your present situation eliminate chaos and bring simplicity?

CHAPTER 12

God First

Pride, at its heart, is an obsession with self.

-Carey Nieuwhof

Order matters.

The last time I assembled furniture, I reached what I had assumed was the end of the project. Only then did I realize I had mistakenly switched two critical components. Without following the ordered steps, my end table would never stand on its own. Unfortunately, I could give several examples of similar occurrences when I have failed to proceed in the proper sequence.

When it comes to navigating through life, even the most free-spirited among us follow basic principles of order. Take driving, for example. What will happen if someone drives east in the westbound lane or runs a red light in the middle of a busy intersection? At the very least, the other drivers will be upset. More than likely, chaos will ensue, and someone will end up seriously injured, or even dead.

In the instances above, the consequences of disorder show up almost immediately. But there are other times when the results of lack of order are not so instantaneous. Consider a home built without following the proper procedure when laying the foundation or constructing the framework. The results may look exceptional, but, over time, problem after problem will appear. Skipping steps and cutting corners may bring temporary success, but it will not last.

The same is true when it comes to our relationship with God.

There is a trap I fall into frequently. I trick myself into thinking I am following God, when, in reality, I am more concerned about *my* desires and *my* way. I go through the motions, doing all the right things, but, ultimately, my heart is in the wrong place. Whether purposefully or unintentionally, I put *my* plans first, then try to fit God into them.

Many times, we think of God as a part of our life, instead of essential to it. We make Him a category on our agendas, squeezing Him into our priorities, right alongside family, career, hobbies, finances, or friendships. The problem with this thinking is that we are attempting to lower God to the level of our control instead of remembering that He is above everything else.

When I get this order wrong, I will struggle to hear God and experience a lack of vision, depressing thoughts, and the desire to quit. I often find myself demeaning and judging others, speaking unkindly, and pushing my agenda, as my life all too quickly overflows with chaos.

James speaks directly to this disorder. Listen to his words: "'God is opposed to the proud, but gives grace to the humble.' Submit, therefore to God. Resist the devil and he will flee from you." (James 4:6-7) There are two ways we can order our lives, and only one is correct. Either God is first, or we are. When God takes precedence, our lives exhibit humility, but if we mistakenly place ourselves first, our lives display pride.

Consider the process of being selected for a team. Do you remember, in school, when two captains would take turns choosing teammates? The first chosen would either be the most athletic or the most popular. All the others hoped only that they would not be one of the last people picked. Though usually not verbalized, the order of the selection indicated that those chosen last were either less valuable to the team or less desired by the captain.

> We find simplicity when we recognize pride and eliminate it from our lives.

While the vast majority of us would say we want God on our side, often our choices place us in direct opposition to Him. By putting ourselves first, we choose pride and inadvertently align ourselves against God. Talk about making life more complicated!

I certainly don't want to set myself in opposition to the God of the universe, and, my guess is, you don't either. We must learn to recognize pride and to make every effort to remove it from our lives.

A study of James, chapters 4-5, gives practical examples of how pride displays itself in our lives. It is present when we are **Fighting with others to get our way (James 4:1-3):** The believers to whom James was writing were frequently quarreling with each other. At the same time, they were wondering why God was not answering their prayers. Their desires were so overpowering that they had become consumed with fighting and destroying one another, instead of loving each other.

We see an example of this type of pride in Mark 10, when two of Jesus' disciples asked Him for an elevated position in His kingdom. They wanted recognition and status that set them apart from the other disciples. When the remaining disciples heard this request, they revealed their own arrogance with a frustrated response. Jesus taught all of them a new paradigm of greatness. He challenged them: "Whoever wishes to become great among you shall be your servant, and whoever wishes to be first among you shall be slave of all. For even the Son of Man did not come to be served, but to serve."[57]

There is a drastic difference between desiring to be great and desiring to be greater than others. In God's kingdom, greatness is achieved by loving God, loving others, and serving well. Anytime we are comparing among ourselves, fighting for status, or putting our agenda first, we can be sure we are walking in pride.

Aligning ourselves with the world, instead of with God (James 4:4): Pride will convince us that we are the exception. Have you ever thought, "I know what God says about _____, but my situation is different," or, "I just don't see what is so bad about _____"? James warns us that establishing a friendship with the world makes us enemies with God. When we compromise God's standards, our behavior implies we know better than Him. Even though we would like to believe we can follow God and the world at the same time, we cannot do so.

In a message known as "the Sermon on the Mount," Jesus cautions against this tendency to compromise, by explaining the impossibility of serving two masters. Loving one master will result in hating the other master, and devotion to one will cause us to despise the other.[58] Dedication to the world, in any area, will set us on a pathway to disdaining God. Our pride tells God that we know better than He does.

Speaking negatively to or about others (James 4:11-12): James advised of the dangers of the tongue in chapter 3 and now continues addressing the problem of speaking negatively regarding followers of Jesus. Anytime I complain against someone else, I display pride, showing I have judged that person, while mistakenly putting myself in God's place.

Jesus also addresses this in the Sermon on the Mount, when He explains how speaking angrily against someone or calling them names makes us guilty before God.[59] He stresses the seriousness of this issue with a warning. If we are attempting to worship God while we knowingly have a conflict with a fellow believer, we should first seek reconciliation before continuing in worship.[60] It takes humility to pursue peace, but pride continues to point out the faults of others.

Boasting about our plans (James 4:13-16): Some of James's readers were bragging about their ideas and the profits those plans would bring. Their confident proclamations about their destiny had them falsely thinking they were in control of it. James reminded them of the brevity of life and how quickly everything could change. When we depend on our own designs and resources, pride takes over. Instead, James instructs us to say, "If the Lord wills, we will live and also do this or that."[61]

I love to have a plan, but, often, my need for making arrangements becomes more important to me than following God. In his book *Hearing God*, Dallas Willard observes, "My extreme preoccupation with knowing God's will for me may only indicate, contrary to what is often thought, that I am overconcerned with myself, not a Christlike interest in the well-being of others or in the glory of God."[62]

While it can be easy to become consumed with where we are headed, focusing too much on the future can be dangerous. Jesus challenges us to "seek first His kingdom and His righteousness" and to believe that "all these things will be added to you." It is enough to trust God for today.[63]

Understanding the right thing to do, but not doing it (James 4:17): James points out that when we know the right thing to do but fail to do it, it becomes a sin to us. A college professor once shared how growing in Christ requires not only ceasing wrong conduct but also implementing positive behavior in its place. When God is at work in our lives, good things will come from it. Jesus put it this way, "For there is no good tree which produces bad fruit, nor, on the other hand, a bad tree which produces good fruit. For each tree is known by its own fruit."[64]

If we are truly following God, our lives will be transformed. We will humbly pursue His direction and produce good fruit. The right thing for you might be helping someone in need, forgiving a person who has wronged you, speaking up for someone else, or giving generously. Whatever it is, if you choose not to do that next right thing, you are choosing your way over God's.

Storing up wealth for ourselves while mistreating others (James 5:1-5): In James's day, the rich were so consumed by collecting more riches that they cheated those who worked for them. Absorbed with self-consumption, they failed to realize the things they were hoarding on earth would never give them pleasure. On the contrary, they were depleting themselves of eternal riches.

Jesus tells the story of a man who modeled this selfish way of life. The man had so much wealth that he decided to build bigger barns to store all of it. He thought he would be satisfied and happy with his riches for many years to come, but he unexpectedly died and lost everything. Jesus warns us this man represents everyone who "stores up treasures for himself but is not rich toward God."[65] Whenever we depend on money to bring satisfaction, to guarantee our comfort or safety, or to provide future security, we are full of pride.

Pride reveals itself in many ways, but one thing remains constant—pride exposes the disorder of our soul. It shows us we are on the path of destruction, moving away from God, while placing our agenda above His.

No matter its form, there is only one antidote for pride, and that is humility. Look at James 4:7 again: "Submit to God. Resist the devil, and he will flee from you." When we recognize pride creeping into or overtaking our life, we need to place ourselves under the authority of God. Doing so begins with repentance, as we turn from our ways and toward His. James describes this process by using words like "cleanse," "purify," "mourn," and "weep." Although it may be painful, repentance is essential to order our lives accordingly.

When we turn away from pride and walk in humility, we are modeling our lives after Jesus. It is in this true humility that we will find the simple life that God designed us to live. But let's be clear. In most cases, the words "simple" and "easy" don't mean the same thing. Sometimes it is easier to submit to God than at other times. When life is going well and we sense God's blessings, it is not hard to place ourselves under His authority. But what about those times when things don't go our way? Those moments when we cannot understand what

God is doing or how He is working?

In chapter two, we discussed the "P" word that many people avoid praying for. While most of us wish we didn't need it, patience and its counterpart, perseverance, are critical to walking in humility. James compares our spiritual patience to a farmer waiting for the land to produce a harvest. The farmer knows that even though he doesn't see immediate results, over time, growth will come. In the same way, we can be patient and wait on God, knowing that He is working, even when we cannot see instantaneous outcomes.[66]

James points us to the life of Job as an example of godly perseverance. Job faithfully followed God and lived with abundant blessings because of it. Then, seemingly out of nowhere, Job's life takes a tragic turn. In short order, he loses his career, his home, his possessions, his children, and his health. Most likely responding from her own grief, Job's wife encourages him to curse God and die. His friends aren't much better, as they accuse him of bringing this disaster upon himself.

At a time when most would have despaired and turned from God, Job continued to persevere. God responded by coming to Job's defense and speaking directly to him, reminding him of His power, character, and presence. Despite the hardships Job was facing, God assured him He was still in control of everything. In the end, God restored Job's fortune and his family, giving Job double the possessions he had previously owned.

Job's story not only reminds us to wait on God patiently; it also shows us the other side of pain. It testifies of God's compassion and encourages us to continue seeking the Lord during our hardest days. No matter the situation, and, regardless of what our circumstances seem to say, God's character does not change. When we don't see life play out the way we want, it does not mean He is not in control. It means it is time to trust God and place ourselves under His authority. Like Job, when we put God first, we can confidently rest in His care.

The battle between self-importance and humility is real. We face it every day. If we follow God only when it is convenient, we reveal a deep-seated pride that believes we know best. Living out of this arrogance will lead us away from God, and we will reap a harvest of chaos and confusion. On the other hand, the path of humility places God first, even when circumstances might challenge us to protect ourselves or to create our own way. Walking in humility sets us on the road to simplicity and ensures we will reap a harvest of peace, joy, and blessing.

Reflection:

1. Which expression of pride do you struggle with the most in your life? Why do you think this is?

2. In what area do you need to put God first? What will that look like for you?

3. Think of someone you know who models humility. How does this humility lead that person on a path of simplicity? What good things do you see coming from that person's life?

CHAPTER 13

The Healing Power of Community

Beneath all our problems, there are desperately
hurting souls that must find the nourishment
only community can provide—or die.
-Larry Crabb, *Connecting*

I am a private person by nature. I easily fall into the trap of thinking I'm not the best conversationalist. Sometimes I rely too much on my own strength and don't think I need the help of others. Without realizing it, I create walls that hold me back from forming connections with people. These walls come from being overconfident in my abilities and can also serve as a protective layer to keep others from inflicting pain upon me. Unfortunately, these barriers can also lead to loneliness and isolation. They not only prevent me from cultivating authentic relationships; they also keep me from growing in my walk with God.

Some of you might question my last statement. Can our

relationships with other people really impact our relationship with God? I'm glad you asked.

As we come to the close of James's letter, we find an intriguing statement: "Therefore, confess your sins to one another, and pray for one another so that you may be healed." (James 5:16) A tip I learned in college is that when you see the word "therefore" in Scripture, you should ask the question: "What is it there for?" Cheesy, I know, but still good advice. Basically, "therefore" signals that the words coming next tie directly to those preceding them. By paying close attention to the flow of the individual thoughts that are shared, we better understand the context of the whole.

If we look back to verses 13-14, we see a series of questions. Each question relates to a real-life situation, followed by practical advice on how to respond:

Question	Response
Is anyone suffering?	Pray.
Is anyone cheerful?	Sing praises.
Is anyone sick?	Call on the leaders of the church to pray over you.

Do you notice the simplicity of James's instructions? It is almost as simple as breathing. If you are suffering, it is natural to pray. Even people who would claim they don't believe in God may find themselves praying when they are faced with traumatic circumstances. If you are cheerful, you will naturally express that cheerfulness. Happy people can't help humming, singing, smiling, or expressing their joy to others. In the same way, when we are sick, we should readily look to our

Christian community for help.

With this last scenario, James's instructions go beyond the sick person and provide guidance for the church leaders to follow, along with a promise of how God will respond. Look at the progression:

Sick Person	Church Leadership	God
Call on the leaders of the church for prayer.	Pray over the sick persons.	Restore those who are sick.
	Anoint the sick persons with oil in the name of the Lord.	Raise them up. Forgive their sins.

Bible scholars debate what type of hardship this sick person is facing. In some verses, this same Greek word is used to refer to physical illness, while, in other verses, it implies spiritual sickness. Scholars also disagree over what it means to anoint someone with oil and how that relates to the church today. The focus on prayer, however, is not debated.

James makes it clear that the "prayer offered in faith" (James 5:15) is what prompts restoration in the sick person. In other words, healing takes place only through the power of prayer.

John Wesley said it well, "God does nothing but in answer to prayer." Maybe you would agree with that statement, but still wonder: "Why do I need other people? Can't I just go straight to God?"

James is showing us that prayer is the language of God's people. Whether we are suffering, cheerful, or sick, prayer should be our normal response. This response is not only for our personal use; it is also part of the natural interaction between Christians. As a believer, I should be praying for and with others and having others pray for me.

Remember where we started with James 5:16, "Therefore, confess your sins to one another, and pray for one another so that you may be healed." On the basis of this natural response to prayer, it only makes sense that when we are sick, whether physically or spiritually, we should look to each other. When we openly express our struggles and receive prayer, we will find that God brings healing to our lives.

> We find simplicity when we experience healing through community.

For most of you reading this, chances are that I don't know you personally. I don't know your challenges or the areas you need to experience God's freedom. I cannot identify the specific healing you long to receive. But I do know that healing comes in community with others.

I shared earlier how I have struggled to make myself vulnerable to developing close relationships. I still have a long way to go, but I am continuing in this journey of learning to pursue God with people instead of isolating myself. It has been an essential catalyst in my spiritual growth.

The first time I became part of an authentic small group changed my life. During my second semester in college, a youth pastor at my home church offered me a proposal. In exchange for an unpaid summer internship working with the students at our church, he and other church leaders would teach and disciple me. Even without pay, I was intrigued and accepted the offer.

That summer, I found myself in a group with other college students who had also agreed to intern. Once a week, we would meet together at the youth pastor's home for Bible study. Now, this was not my first experience in a small group. I had grown up as a part of church life and went to Sunday school classes. I had attended a youth group and even a small group in college, but, somehow, this time was different. This group was authentic and real. The relationships and the things I learned from others shaped, challenged, and changed me. It's not that I didn't learn from the other groups or that the people in those groups were not genuine. But, this time, I reacted differently. I opened up and let down some walls.

Each week, as we gathered, we talked about real things happening in our lives. We discussed what God was doing or what we wanted Him to do, things we were learning and what we were confused about, how we were growing or the areas where we needed to continue to grow. During one particular meeting, the leader asked us to share how we had heard from God that week. As we took turns, one person admitted he was struggling to see God and to hear from Him. This level of honesty helped me realize that it is okay not to have all the answers and that it is also okay to admit our shortcomings to others. In this group, I found the healing power of community—something that I desperately needed but that I wasn't even aware I was missing.

Fast forward about ten years. One of my biggest challenges came when I entered a leadership role. While people approached me for advice or counsel, I seldom sought counsel for myself. I wasn't comfortable sharing my struggles. I didn't know who was a safe person to confide my concerns with or even what was appropriate to share. In my uncertainty, I again erected walls, and, as a result, I became isolated.

My choice to isolate myself added unnecessary pain and confusion in my life. Even though people surrounded me, I felt alone. I struggled to find friends, and I wasn't sure how to open up and share with the few I did have. Although I was helping other people to grow spiritually, my own walk with God was declining.

During this season, God reminded me of the words from James 5:15. I needed to "confess my sins" to other people, and I needed their support and prayers to find healing. My breakthrough was contingent on my openness. As God spoke to me, I committed to sharing both my dreams and my struggles with a few, trusted friends.

Even as I write this, the names of four friends spring to mind. These are people like me (and maybe you) who struggle to share their pain but who are determined to grow. I have sat many hours with each of them—telling them what is going on in my life, listening as they share what is happening in theirs, and then together coming into God's presence and pouring out our hearts. These are the friends who truly know me, who pray for me regularly, who encourage me when I am down, who fight for me, who challenge me, who check on me, and who walk with me. Without these women, I would not be who I am today.

Looking back, it scares me to think about how I almost overlooked such vital friendships. My walls and my pride were telling me I could not find authentic community in my everyday circles, and I almost missed out on what was right in front of me.

Despite what you tell yourself, you cannot grow in spiritual maturity without others. You might be able to grow intellectually or to develop a skill, but real growth involves deep internal work that God designed us to do in relationships with each other.

Earlier this year, I worked with a team of women from my church to organize a women's event called *Breakthrough to Freedom*. The name for this event was birthed from a time of prayer and seeking God. As we asked God what the women needed, the word "freedom" dominated our thoughts. We believed God wanted women to experience a breakthrough on their spiritual journeys, beginning with each of us. Over the next several months, God answered our prayers. Every single woman on the team experienced new levels of freedom in her life.

Going into the event, we were excited to see how God would continue to work. One of the most significant parts of that day was a panel consisting of multiple team members. Each woman, many of them for the first time, publicly shared her journey to freedom. These beautiful women genuinely and openly told how God had healed (or was currently in the process of healing) them in their struggles through unforgiveness, anxiety, pride, sexual addiction, abortion, and much more.

If you asked these brave women, I know that each of them would tell you that sharing their stories brought a new level of healing and deepened their walk with God. Not only did they experience this transformation personally; they also helped other women experience healing. To encourage those attending the event to embrace community, to share their stories, and to move toward freedom, we included some guidelines in the conference materials. I'm restating them here, in hopes they will encourage you, too:

"The Bible teaches us that healing comes through community. An important step in your journey of restoration is sharing your whole story, holding nothing back. Though it can sound terrifying, the truth is that powerful healing can come through sharing our hurt, pain, mistakes, and fears.

Here are some tips to help you:

- Before you share with people, talk with God about it. He is our Healer; He knows everything about us; and He loves us unconditionally. Remember that you can be honest with God because He is already aware of your thoughts, emotions, and fears.

- There are some parts of your story that you should only share with one or two people. Find someone whom you trust implicitly, who won't judge you, and who cares about your spiritual development.

- It can be powerful to share your story in a group setting. When you do, remember you don't need to share everything. First of all, not everything is appropriate to mention, and if you share your whole life story, it will take forever!

- Think about what you want the people you are sharing with to know, and concentrate on that specific theme, time frame, or part of your journey.

- Be honest. Give a real picture, but don't exaggerate what happened to you to make it more dramatic.

- Be careful how you speak about other people. Take responsibility for your actions, and avoid assigning motives or emotions to other people.

- As you find healing through sharing your story, help others do the same. Give the same care you want to receive. Listen, encourage, and be an advocate for other's freedom."

It is my hope and prayer that each one of you reading this book will take a step forward into deeper relationships with other believers. I realize that some of you have opened up before and may have been hurt or rejected. It can be easy to project our past experiences onto our future, but I hope you will guard against it. If we are not careful, we can allow our past, our insecurities, and our fears to rob us of finding the healing power of community God has designed for us today.

In his book *Soul Care*, Rob Reimer says, "There is no freedom without honesty; there is no breakthrough without brokenness."[67] If you are struggling to grow spiritually or feel like you are stuck or even going backward, you need community. Without it, you will never learn to live like Jesus or become all that God wants you to be.

Maybe all of this sounds great, but you are not sure where to get started. Let me encourage you to be careful not to overwhelm yourself to the point you never move forward. Change takes time. Start by thinking about one simple thing you can do, and do that. Then do the next thing. Then the next. And the next.

Here are a few ideas of what this might look like:

- Schedule a coffee or lunch date with a friend or a potential friend. Share what is happening in your life, including a few of your questions or struggles. You don't have to talk about everything, but start by sharing something.

- Host a dinner, and invite some people you respect spiritually. Think of a good question or two you can throw into the discussion that will help foster a productive conversation.

- Find one or two friends you can pray with regularly. Set aside time to discuss what you each need prayer for, and talk to God together.

- Meet with a mentor, spiritual leader, or counselor. Listen to their advice and commit to putting it into practice.

- If you are in a church or organization that has a prayer team or dedicated prayer time, share your needs, and allow others to pray with you.

- If you are not part of a church, visit a church this week. If you already attend a church, visit a small group. Remember that churches and groups have personalities, so you may need to try a few before you find a good fit.

- If you are in a group, commit to participate in the discussion. Don't be afraid to tackle some hard questions. Admit when you don't understand, when you are struggling, or when you need input from others.

Whatever you choose next, don't rely on someone else to take the first step. Consider that maybe God wants to use you to be the catalyst for building community with those around you.

I love what my pastor regularly reminds our church, "In isolation, I become who I want to be. In community, I become who God wants me to be."

So who does God want you to be? And what steps do you need to take to move forward toward that vision?

Reflection:

1. Share about a time God used other believers to help you grow.

2. What barriers have you put up that are keeping you from finding the healing power of community? How have those barriers negatively affected you?

3. How can you become a catalyst for building relationships where you live?

4. What is one thing you will do this week to take steps toward embracing healthy relationships?

CHAPTER 14

Releasing God's Power

You can do more than pray after you have prayed. But you
cannot do more than pray until you have prayed.

-S. D. Gordon, *Quiet Talks on Prayer*

One evening, shortly after I had rearranged my furniture, I noticed the lamp on my nightstand had begun to flicker. A few nights later, the bulb flashed brightly, before going out completely. Unable to see, I set my book on the stand, and, interestingly enough, the light came back on. So the next time it went out, I hit the nightstand with my hand, and the light returned. This scenario continued for some time—the lamp would flicker and go out; then I would smack the stand to correct the problem.

Each time I went through this cycle, I wondered what was wrong with this lamp (and why I kept forgetting to buy a new one). Eventually, one night, the light went out, and, despite my best smacking efforts, would not turn back on. At this point, I switched on my overhead light and picked up the lamp.

Examining it more closely, I made an important discovery—the bulb was loose. The problem was not with my lamp at all. It was merely a problem with the connection.

For weeks, I had thought I needed a new lamp, when, in reality, I just needed to ensure it was connected correctly to the source of light. As quickly as I made this discovery, I sensed God speaking to me. Similar to my lamp fiasco, I often find myself frustrated and blaming God for my lack of spiritual power, when the real problem is not with God at all.

> We find simplicity when we call on God's power through prayer.

God is the source of all spiritual power, and we tap into that power through prayer. Do you remember how James challenged his readers that they did not have because they did not ask?[68] The same is true for us. If we fail to pray and to ask for God's intervention, we will not see His power in our lives.

The gospel of Mark, chapter 9, gives a perfect example of this, as we observe Jesus' disciples suffering a lack of power directly because of their lack of prayer. I can't help relating to their struggle. They were following Jesus, wanting to serve Him and to help people, but something was holding them back.

During this particular instance, a father came to the disciples, begging them to help his young son. An evil spirit possessed the boy, causing him to be mute and to experience seizures. While a crowd gathered, watching to see what would happen, the disciples tried to assist him. They wanted to heal him, but they could not do it. They must have felt embarrassed and frustrated at their inability to help, especially in front of so many people.

In complete contrast to the disciples, Jesus entered the scene and immediately healed the boy. We don't have to wonder what the disciples were thinking now, because Mark tells us. They wanted to know why they were unable to drive out the demon. How could Jesus so easily do what they had failed to accomplish?

There was clearly a disconnect between the disciples and the power of God. Even though they wanted to see God work and perform miracles, they lacked His authority and might. Do you ever feel that way? With a desire to serve Jesus, to love and help others, but lacking the power of God? As if no matter how hard you try, something seems missing.

Jesus' answer to His disciples' question was simple, "This kind cannot come out by anything but prayer."[69] The problem was that the disciples wanted the *power* of God without *depending* on God. Likewise, seeing miracles displayed through our lives requires prayer.

Maybe this sounds too simple, but I wonder how often we are frustrated with things solely because we have neglected to pray. Charles Spurgeon was known for saying, "Whether we like it or not, asking is the rule of the kingdom." Jesus taught, through His words and example, that prayer and God's power are directly connected.

In the previous chapter, we learned that prayer is the natural communication of God's people. James continues this teaching with a profound statement: "The effective prayer of a righteous person can accomplish much." (James 5:15) Do you believe that God hears you when you pray and that your prayers can accomplish astounding things?

Many of us underestimate how effectively God can work

through our prayers. James seems to have that impression, too, because, right after his statement about our prayers accomplishing much, he points us to the example of the prophet Elijah. If you are unfamiliar with Elijah, he was a prophet and a notable figure in Jewish history. While the Old Testament records many of Elijah's adventures, James focuses on one particular highlight. Once, Elijah prayed for it to stop raining, and it did—for three and a half years! Then, he prayed again, asking for the rains to come, and showers returned in abundance.

There's no question that Elijah was a man who heard from God directly and who spoke on God's behalf. When he prayed, he changed history, performing miracle after miracle. I have a tendency to put men and women like Elijah in a separate category from myself, thinking they have a special anointing from God far different from my experience. Sometimes I'm tempted to believe that the kind of miracles Elijah saw don't still happen today. But look at how James makes a connection between our lives and Elijah's life: "Elijah was a man *with a nature like ours.*" (James 5:17, emphasis added) In case you want to put Elijah on a pedestal, don't do so. He was just like you and me.

How is this possible?

Because the power of Elijah's prayer had nothing to do with who Elijah was and everything to do with who God is.

The same is true for us. Prayer is not about how good, capable, or magnificent we are; prayer centers on God's goodness, capabilities, and magnificence. I love how R. A. Torrey puts it: "The only limit to what prayer can do is what God can do. But all things are possible with God (Matthew 19:26); therefore, prayer is omnipotent."[70] In other words, prayer is all-powerful because when we pray, we are tapping into an omnipotent and invincible source.

Honestly, prayer is challenging for me. I struggle with distractions and doubts, and I wrestle with feelings of inadequacy. But, simultaneously, I see God perform undeniable wonders through prayer. Even though it can be difficult to pray, I have found that the more I pray, the more I see God's power released in my life.

Last year, I had the opportunity to travel with a team to Mexico to visit a ministry called "Seedtime and Harvest." We were in an area with a heavy drug-cartel presence and a struggling economy, yet I sensed God's remarkable power. The church leaders were bold and courageous, while, at the same time, peaceful and filled with joy. They loved their community and were seeing many people find freedom in Jesus.

During our visit, we attended several church services. I wish I could have captured the experience and somehow downloaded it to share with you. The worship was energetic, the people were eager to learn, and there was a sense of anticipation that God would move.

Toward the end of each service, there was a call for prayer. Our team was asked to go to the front of the sanctuary and pray one-on-one over people who came forward. Standing there, I watched, as person after person flooded to the front of the room, and I began to feel inadequate. My Spanish is extremely limited, and most of the people in attendance did not speak English. How would I know what to pray? Would my prayers make a difference? How could God use me?

I uttered a quick prayer asking for God's help, before placing my hands on the lady in front of me. Suddenly, when I began to pray out loud, something shifted. Despite the language barrier, God showed me how to pray. As I prayed for each person, I had what I can only describe as a supernatural understanding of and a love for these women. Just like those of Elijah, my prayers connected to the power of God, filling me with faith and the belief that God would answer them.

I know I am not the only one who is learning and growing in prayer. When you think of praying, what barriers do you face?

- Lack of knowledge and experience?

- Feelings of inadequacy?

- Busy schedule?

- Lack of energy?

- Fear of praying out loud?

- Being overwhelmed by the needs?

- Doubt?

- Trying without seeing results?

No matter what obstacle you struggle to overcome, I encourage you to press through it. Prayer is not about having it all together; it is about communicating with the One who does.

Let's specifically address the barrier of "trying without seeing results." Maybe you have tried to pray, but it seems God doesn't hear you. Perhaps you asked for a particular thing, but there is no change in the situation. When this happens, it can be easy to give up.

If prayer has been a difficult or discouraging experience for you, I want to point you to a few considerations from James. First, consider that you may not be praying for the right things. If we look again at James 4:3, we learn that when we pray out of selfishness or impure motives, we will not see God move. If your prayer centers on getting what you want or making yourself great, don't expect God to honor that request, either. Prayer is about releasing God's power, not about making us feel good.

Examine your motives. Why are you praying? What is your desire? Are you seeking to elevate yourself or to proclaim God's greatness?

Second, understand that the goal of prayer is not to predict the future. As we saw in James 4:14-16, boasting about our plans and where we are heading in life does not please God. Often, we are looking for God either to give us a life plan or to affirm the life plan we have created for ourselves. God is not a fortune teller. Instead, He wants us to do the right thing, right now. As you pray, look for God's guidance for today and not merely focus on where you want to be in the future.

Third, remember that God does not always function according to our timetable. As we have already established, patience is a primary factor in His kingdom. While we mostly focus on immediate results, God is concerned with the process. There are seasons of life when He may seem silent, but He is actually accomplishing something deep in us. Even if we don't have eyes to see it at the time, when you don't view the results you think you should, don't write off God. Instead, keep praying, trusting that He is at work.

Lastly, don't forget that God's priorities are usually different from yours and mine. Think back to the very beginning of James, when we looked at how the trials we face are developing character in our lives. Maybe you are asking God to remove the very situation He designed to help you grow.

Perhaps you are ignoring the steps toward maturity that God wants you to take.

God desires His children to live the same life of simplicity that Jesus lived. One that comes when we allow God to set our priorities and to change our perspectives. But this simple life can be achieved only through depending on His power entirely.

So what about you?

Do you depend on God?

Do you pray for Him to give you wisdom and insight and to make you more like Jesus?

Are you tapping into the only real source of power through prayer?

Reflection:

1. How can you tell the difference between depending on yourself and depending on God?

2. Recall a time when you saw God's power as a result of praying. What did that look like? What made this significant?

3. What is your most challenging barrier to praying? What practical steps can you take to overcome it?

4. What do you need to pray about today? Whom do you need to pray for?

CHAPTER 15

Your Impact

Not only did God create you to live in this particular season,
but He gave you just the right personality, abilities, talents, and
gifts to accomplish what you are called to do. You are not an
accident. You are here on purpose for a purpose.

-Chris Hodges, *The Daniel Dilemma*

I have studied through James many times, and as I would
come to the last two verses, I wasn't sure what to make of
them. Most of the time, I skipped over them, without giving
too much thought to how they applied to my life. Writing this
book has caused me to evaluate things more closely.

James's closing words state: "My brethren, if any among
you strays from the truth and one turns him back, let him
know that he who turns a sinner from the error of his way will
save his soul from death and will cover a multitude of sins."
(James 5:19-20) This time, as I studied and prayed, a new
insight seemed to jump off the page—when we live as Jesus
lived, we will always impact the people around us.

When I study the Bible, I am mostly looking for answers to my questions and solutions to my problems. I tend to think through everything from the perspective of my experience and my needs. Here, James reminds us that while learning to embrace God's principles will undoubtedly change us, it does not stop there.

What God is doing in me is never just about me. The truth I am learning not only has the power to impact me; it also has the potential to influence others through me. Our journey of learning to live like Jesus and to embrace the simplicity He offers allows us to participate in a mission much greater than ourselves.

As Jesus walked this earth, He had a clear purpose, as stated immediately following what might be the best-known verse in the Bible, John 3:16: "For God so loved the world, that He gave His only begotten Son, that whoever believes in Him shall not perish, but have eternal life." Reading into the next verse, we see His objective: "For God did not send the Son into the world to judge the world, but that the world might be saved through Him."[71]

Jesus came to offer hope and healing to the broken and the hurting. He came to seek and to save the lost. Our purpose comes through joining Jesus in living out His purpose.

As I am writing this chapter, my church is going through a sermon series called "Out of Commission." We are learning how God's children are called to live "on mission" with Him, yet often we get "off mission."

Nothing gets me "out of commission" more often than feeling insignificant. I look at the world around me, and I wonder how I can make an impact. There are times I sit in airports or other public places and watch hundreds or even thousands of people pass by, and I realize I don't know a single one of them. And they don't know me.

Sometimes I can get so caught up in thinking that, to make a difference, I need a bigger platform, a higher position, more financial resources, or a deeper walk with God. But this type of thinking does not line up with His.

If we truly love God, we will grow in our maturity and share that love with others. He will use us to lead people into a closer relationship with Him, and we will see His transformational power at work right where we live. On the other hand, if we believe the lie that God cannot use us, we will experience internal wrestling and a lack of peace, falling short in fulfilling His call on our lives.

Satan would like nothing more than to deceive you into thinking you don't know enough or aren't good enough or aren't mature enough to make an impact. The truth is that if God can work *in* you, He can work *through* you. I have heard it said, "Don't let what you can't do stop you from doing what you can do." God is calling each of us to be on mission with Him right where we are, and He doesn't want anything to hold us back—least of all, ourselves.

> We find simplicity when we live out God's mission right where we are.

As Jesus walked this earth, He had time for people. He moved slowly through the crowds, ministering to the masses, but He also ministered to the one. Jesus not only talked about God's love; He also shared God's love in a practical way everywhere He went, with everyone He met.

Like Jesus, you live in a complicated world filled with

hurting people looking for hope. No matter your circumstances, where you live or what you do for a living—your mission is to share that hope. Don't wait for the perfect situation to present itself. Look around you, pay attention, and love the one right in front of you.

As we find simplicity through modeling our life after Jesus, not only will we find our purpose; we will also lead others to discover theirs.

Reflection

1. What is holding you back from fully living out God's mission?
2. Whom can you offer hope to today?
3. What is your next step on the journey to finding simplicity and to learning to live as Jesus lived?

Thank You

To each lady who walked through the book of James with me in a small group setting—thank you! The lessons we learned together laid the foundation for this book. I am grateful for your honesty, your vulnerability, and your friendship.

Barb, thank you for embracing the writing journey with me. Your heart and insights are woven into every page of this book. Like me, *Finding Simplicity* was not just a project you were working on; it was also a truth you were learning to live day by day. Your friendship, encouragement, wisdom, and talent are treasured gifts.

Dad and Mom, you are, and have always been, my biggest encouragers. Thank you for always believing in me, challenging me, and helping me continue to dream.

Pastor Gabe and Pastor Victor, thank you for reviewing my manuscript. Not only was your insight helpful in the writing process, but your support all along my speaking and writing journey means more than you know.

Endnotes

Introduction
1 John Ortberg, *The Life You've Always Wanted: Spirtual Disciples for Ordinary People* (Grand Rapids: Zondervan, 2002), 79.

Chapter 1
2 Douglas Moo, *James* (Downers Grove, IL: InterVarsity Press, 2015), 60.
3 Acts 11:19.

Chapter 2
4 James 1:4.
5 1 Corinthians 13:11-12.
6 Luke 2:52.
7 Samuel Chand, *Leadership Pain* (Nashville: Thomas Nelson, 2015), 93.

Chapter 3
8 Emily Steele Elliott, *Expectation Corner: Or Adam Slowman, Is Your Door Open?* (Merchant Books, 2013), 6.
9 Ephesians 1:3
10 *Expectation Corner*, 11.

Chapter 4
11 Matthew 14:27.
12 Matthew 14:31.

Chapter 5
13 Genesis 2:16-17.
14 Genesis 3:12.
15 Genesis 3:13.
16 Matthew 4:4.
17 Matthew 4:7.
18 Matthew 4:10.

Chapter 6
19 2 Timothy 3:16.
20 Hebrews 4:12.
21 Joshua 1:7-8.
22 Hebrews 2:1.
23 Proverbs 30:5.
24 Psalm 19:7.
25 Psalm 1:2-3.
26 Matthew 7:13-14.

Chapter 7
27 Eugene H. Peterson, *Eat This Book: A Conversation in the Art of Spiritual Reading* (Grand Rapids: William B. Eerdmans Publishing Company, 2006), 18.

Chapter 8
28 John MacArthur, *The MacArthur New Testament Commentary: James* (Chicago: Moody Publishers, 1998), 98.
29 Colossians 3:15.
30 I Thessalonians 4:9-10.
31 I Corinthians 13:1-3.
32 I Corinthians 13:13.
33 I John 2:1-11.
34 2 Peter 1:7-8.
35 Luke 10:25.
36 Luke 10:27.
37 Luke 10:29.

38 Luke 10:36.

39 Galatians 3:28.

Chapter 9

40 Hebrews 11:1.

41 James 2:22.

42 Joshua 1:2.

Chapter 10

43 1 Samuel 25:10-11.

Chapter 11

44 Proverbs 1:7.

45 Proverbs 2:4.

46 Proverbs 3:14.

47 Proverbs 3:17-18.

48 Proverbs 3:8.

49 Proverbs 3:4.

50 Proverbs 3:23.

51 Proverbs 5:1-3.

52 Proverbs 9:4.

53 Proverbs 9:16.

54 Proverbs 9:13.

55 1 Corinthians 1:24.

56 Luke 6:12-13.

Chapter 12

57 Mark 10:43-45.

58 Matthew 6:24.

59 Matthew 6:22.

60 Matthew 5:23-24.

61 James 4:16.

62 Dallas Willard, *Hearing God: Developing a Conversational Relationship with God* (Downers Grove, IL: IVP Books, 2012), 33.

63 Matthew 6:32.
64 Luke 6:43-44.
65 Luke 12:21.
66 James 5:7-8.

Chapter 13
67 Dr. Rob Reimer, *Soul Care: 7 Transformational Principles for a Healthy Soul* (Franklin, TN: Carpenter's Son Publishing, 2016), 82.

Chapter 14
68 James 4:2.
69 Mark 9:29.
70 R. A. Torrey, *God's Power in Your Life* (New Kensington, PA: Whitaker House, 1982), 94.

Chapter 15
71 John 3:17.

About the Author

Amber Parker is a writer and speaker who helps others activate their faith and go deeper in their walk with God. She serves as the VP of Staff Development at Advancing Native Missions, a global-missions organization. Amber enjoys teaching, coaching leaders, and building teams both here in the United States and around the world.

When she is not working, you will probably find Amber enjoying the mountain views in her small Virginia town, trying out a new recipe in the kitchen, curled up with a good book, or in deep conversation with a friend.

Find out more at amberparker.net.

GLOBAL MISSIONS HAS CHANGED. FIND OUT HOW.

ANM is building a worldwide movement focused on giving everyone everywhere access to the gospel of Jesus Christ. Instead of sending American missionaries to other countries, we partner with local Christians serving in their home countries, where they are the most economical and often the most effective workers for God's kingdom. Through partnership with ANM, Christians in the U.S. can participate in global missions from their own backyard and make a meaningful difference in lives around the world. God is at work in the world. **Join Him – *'til all hear!***

ANM | ADVANCING NATIVE MISSIONS

You can learn more at **advancingnativemissions.com**
Email: **contact@advancingnativemissions.com**